Best of Breed

THE BORDER TERRIER

Your Essential Guide
From Puppy To
Senior Dog

Edited By

Betty Judge

ACKNOWLEDGEMENTS

The publishers would like to acknowledge the following for help with photography: Hearing Dogs for Deaf People, Pets As Therapy, Betty Judge (Plushcourt), Marie Sharp (Rhozzum), Lesley Gosling (Akenside), Jayne Gillam (Orenberg), Lorraine Drew and her daughter, Ruth, Dawn Bladen (Emblehope), Stewart McPherson (Brumberhill), Ronnie Wilkinson (Otterkin), Anne Roslin-Williams (Mansergh), Joyce Martin, and Karen Grace.

Cover photo: © Tracy Morgan Animal Photography (www.animalphotographer.co.uk)
pages 21 and 58 © istockphoto.com/Mark Bond; page 62 © istockphoto.com/Eric Isselee;
pages 70 and 73 © istockphoto.com/Owen Price; page 125 © istockphoto.com/Griselda Amorim

The BritisThe British Breed Standard reproduced in Chapter 7 is the copyright of the Kennel Club and published with the club's kind permission. Extracts from the American Breed Standard are reproduced by kind permission of the American Kennel Club.

THE QUESTION OF GENDER
The 'he' pronoun is used throughout this book instead of the rather impersonal 'it', but no gender bias is intended.

First published in 2008 by The Pet Book Publishing Company Limited
St Martin's Farm, Chapel Lane, Zeals, Warminster, BA12 6NZ
Reprinted in 2009, 2010, 2011, 2012, 2015 and 2018.

© 2008 and 2018 Pet Book Publishing Company Limited.

Printed by Printworks Global Ltd., London & Hong Kong

CONTENTS

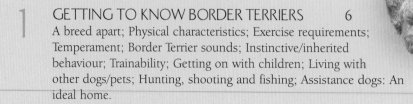

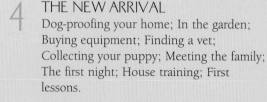

GETTING TO KNOW BORDER TERRIERS

Chapter 1

The Border Terrier is an old established breed of terrier, named after the Border Terrier Hunt, which used this type of terrier, along with Foxhounds, to hunt along the Scottish/English border in country that is mostly hill and open moorland. The terriers were required to follow the horses on the hunts and to dislodge the fox from its earth. The 'earth' is perhaps a misnomer for the rocky places where the foxes take refuge in this type of countryside.

These activities in the past have shaped what we know today as the Border Terrier. They have shaped the breed physically and mentally, and the traits required in those rugged working dogs have ensured the Border Terrier's ever-increasing popularity today.

A BREED APART
Take a Border Terrier for a walk almost anywhere and you will be approached by someone saying, "Oh, a Border Terrier! My father/grandmother/friend used to have one." There is a camaraderie among Border Terrier owners, as if we share a well-kept secret – knowing what a wonderful breed it is. The breed has become more publicised in recent years with appearances on television and film, and with high-profile celebrities owning the breed. Vets frequently own Border Terriers and recommend the breed to their clients because of their inherent healthiness and equable temperament.

Border Terriers (and usually their owners, too) are sociable, and seem to recognise their own kind. I was told of two Border Terrier owners from the middle of England who met on a remote Cornish beach. They got chatting and were delighted

There is something very special about the Border Terrier that sets him apart from other dog breeds.

7

Grizzle and tan: The hairs are banded in dark tips, and the shade may vary from light red to almost blue in colour.

to discover that their Border Terriers were, in fact, brothers.

PHYSICAL CHARACTERISTICS

What makes the Border Terrier instantly recognisable, be it bandbox smart or doormat scruffy, is its otter-like head. This is shorter in the muzzle compared with the ubiquitous Jack Russell, and blunter in shape. The eyes are dark and look at you with intelligence. The head is framed by small, dark, velvet ears (though these are often more mohair than velvet if left to their own devices). The legs are longer than the average Jack Russell, as befit a terrier who had to travel across rough, heather-covered terrain in the Borders countryside.

A small dog, about 30-35 cm high (12-15 inches), the Border Terrier is lithe rather than stocky – remember those rocky crevasses into which he had to creep. He has a full tail – which is never docked – but not so long that its tip could get damaged. The Border Terrier may be less than knee high, but he has a 'big dog' character; he is a dog you own with pride.

COAT AND COLOURS

The Border Terrier is covered in a rough coat of various hues, from rich foxy red through to pale brown, all covered by the terms 'grizzle and tan' or 'red'. He might be what is called a 'blue and tan' colour, which is not so common but equally correct. A blue and tan puppy starts out being black with tan legs, but at maturity the black hairs develop white sections, which gives the overall appearance of a bluish colour.

The colour of a Border Terrier is not constant: if he is hand-stripped correctly, the new coat

Blue and tan: The mixture of black hairs, silver hairs and silver hairs with black tips gives the 'blue' colour.

grows through bright like new paint. As the coat grows, the colour fades until it is very pale and is ready to be stripped out again.

A wheaten-coloured Border Terrier is a very rare sight indeed – he has no black hairs anywhere, and his ears are a pale blue colour. This colour is the result of a recessive gene that is thought to have died out. Border Terriers that have had their coats cut off (a heinous crime unless the dog is very elderly), grow a soft coat of this pale wheaten hair, so don't get too excited if you see one of this rare colour.

The texture of the coat is coarse; one Border Terrier I knew was nicknamed 'Brillo' at scout camp because of his grizzled wiry coat. The top wiry coat covers an undercoat of softer hair, which gives efficient insulation from wintry weather and from the full blast of an open fire in the home, which is a Border Terrier's favourite place to lie.

The coat needs stripping off by hand twice a year, which is a job for the owner rather than the grooming parlour. A weekly brush will help keep some of the undercoat off the carpets and furniture.

EXERCISE REQUIREMENTS

If you appreciate that the original Border Terrier put in huge mileages during a working day, you will realise that the average pet dog is never going to get enough exercise. Their stamina is phenomenal, but they can be perfectly fit and contented without going to extremes.

Obviously, first thing in the morning, a walk or a run in the garden is essential for toilet purposes, and the same at night

WEIGHED IN

The weight of a Border Terrier should be 5.9-7.1 kg for males (13-15 lb) and 5.1-6.4 kg for bitches (11-14 lb) These weights were set down by the breed club in the 1920s and reflect what is the ideal weight for a Border Terrier in fit condition. Nowadays, our children and our dogs have both benefited from improved diets, so the average weights today are probably above the ideals. The build of a Border Terrier is more Whippet than Labrador, so if your Border Terrier is verging on the latter, a reduction in food plus more exercise is probably required.

The Border Terrier is built for endurance and will happily keep going all day long.

before retiring. What happens in between varies so much that it is impossible to generalise – some Border Terriers are lucky enough to get an interesting, free-running period in the local park, others have to be content with a walk round the block on a lead. The Border Terrier is nothing if not adaptable, but he does best when his mind and muscles are both exercised.

Border Terriers have an excellent sense of smell, which they use to the full during exercise. A fall of snow shows us what they 'see' with their noses: tracks of rabbit, fox, or badger – all wonderful 'sights' for a Border Terrier. Using an extending lead should enable all dogs to experience freedom to explore their environment safely. The Border Terrier is not a sedentary lap dog and he should never be treated as one.

TEMPERAMENT

Temperament as well as physical make-up was determined by life with the Border hunt. The terriers lived with hounds, so a quarrelsome nature was definitely out of the question. All dogs are descended from pack animals, and Border Terriers are no different, but their pack instinct has been tempered by their need to exert a bit of independence. A Border Terrier has to think out things for himself when working underground, and perhaps had to find his own way home after a day's hunt.

LEADERSHIP ISSUES

A Border Terrier today likes to be a member of a pack, even though the pack usually consists only of human beings! He likes there to be a pack leader, and can suss out within minutes who is the leader in his household. This is not necessarily the person issuing the orders, but the one who exudes a calm sense of authority.

In some households, the dog is treated as if he is the leader of the pack, and as this is not a role all dogs take to, conflict and bad behaviour ensues. If a Border Terrier is promoted to pack leader, he will take upon himself the role of leader to guard his pack members, to see off intruders, human and canine. He will, in other words, be a complete nuisance. Among my own pack there is a pecking order, and the highest dog is greeted by the others with much tail-wagging and face licking, which he accepts with quiet dignity. As I am pack leader, I too get greeted in a similar manner, and I reinforce my position by accepting the attention.

Bred to work underground, with no direction, the Border Terrier is a dog who thinks for himself.

BORDER TERRIER BEHAVIOUR

Border Terriers are sociable dogs, not by nature aggressive, but will defend themselves if attacked. They can be biddable or obstinate – whichever suits them best at the time. If there is a food treat on offer, a Border Terrier will obey quickly; if there is a more attractive scent to follow, then that has priority. This is an intelligent dog that is quick to learn, but he often gets bored with repetitious training.

Some strains of Border Terrier are more excitable than others, but, with suitable management and training, their energy can be channelled so that they fit into family activities. A Border Terrier puppy needs to be socialised with other dogs at the earliest age possible so that he doesn't grow up with an inflated idea of his own importance. Breeders who keep several Border Terriers have an advantage here, for they are able to let their puppies mix with the adults from an early age.

Two Border Terriers can live together in harmony but the best practice is to start with one and wait until he/she is behaving in a civilised manner before obtaining a second. Sometimes, two's company, three's a crowd. If two Border Terriers fall out with each other, it is very difficult to get them to accept each other again.

BORDER TERRIER

Border Terriers get on well together – but it is better to start with one and add another when your first dog is fully trained.

BORDER TERRIER SOUNDS

I am often asked: "Are Border Terriers noisy?" In the past, a terrier was required to have a voice, which it used when working underground, letting his handler know by the sounds coming up through the ground what was happening. Nowadays, terrier men use electronic locators to give them some information from several feet underground.

A Border Terrier's bark tells several different stories. There is the excited bark when a walk or food is imminent; a warning bark when their sharp hearing detects the gate latch being moved and someone is coming. Then there is the lovely 'singing' – a wolf-like howl, which they all join in with, producing a melodious chorus of bass, tenor and soprano voices. This seems to reinforce the pack's identity, and some say it harks back to the days when Border Terriers lived with packhounds – although it is debatable whether learned behaviour can be inherited.

What we do not get with Border Terriers is the continuous, mindless yapping of some terrier breeds. Visitors to my kennel are surprised by the peace that follows the initial excitement. A Border Terrier does not usually bark without a reason – although the reason might not always be obvious to their owner. A Border Terrier will bark when something is different: "That plant-pot wasn't there yesterday", and they will bark at a scent: "There's been a strange dog about!" One of my dogs was missing after a walk, but was heard barking in the distance. Eventually, we went to him, and there he was, letting us know that, out of our sight, a heifer had fallen into a brook and couldn't get out.

INSTINCTIVE/INHERITED BEHAVIOUR

Prospective Border Terrier owners should be aware that this breed has a full set of instincts present, which, in the dim and distant past, would have equipped it for survival. Thus a Border Terrier will spot a prey species – a rabbit, cat, squirrel etc – and he will stalk it, chase it, catch it, kill it, and finally eat it.

Other breeds do not have a full set of instincts; some of the stages may have been bred out. For instance, the working sheepdog goes through the first three stages: seeing, stalking, chasing, but he neither catches, kills nor eats his prey species, the sheep. A gundog has all instincts present, except the killing and eating stages.

A Border Terrier can be taught not to chase sheep, but I have never tried to stop one chasing rabbits, because I feel I would be wasting my time. A Border Terrier will often live happily with the family cat, but, outside the home, other cats are fair game in a Border Terrier's mind.

SENSITIVE SIDE

Considering their courage and gameness to tackle a fox, Border Terriers are quite sensitive dogs, and like to do the right thing for their owners. A Border Terrier does not like to be shouted at, perhaps because of his sensitive hearing. I always speak quietly to my dogs, and if I need to raise my voice, they are so surprised that they obey instantly – this could be a life-saver if a dangerous situation arose. A Border Terrier will also sulk if he is reprimanded sternly.

Border Terriers have a stoical attitude to pain and are careful never to show any injury. This makes life incredibly difficult unless the owner is very attuned to the behaviour and expression of their Border Terrier.

A Border Terrier has a full set of instincts, and, given the opportunity, he will see, stalk, chase, catch and kill his prey.

GOING UNDERGROUND

Being essentially a working terrier, the Border Terrier does have the instinct to creep into holes in the ground, which may, or may not, be inhabited by other creatures. This curiosity is often fuelled by watching other terriers at work. A lone Border Terrier will rarely get himself into trouble going to ground, which is a fear that many prospective owners have. Most Border Terriers are cautious, and, if confronted with something underground that they are unsure of, will back out.

The presence of another terrier is a different matter, and two terriers will egg each other on, and the outcome is far from certain. If your Border Terrier does disappear underground, the best way to extract him is to move away and keep quiet. Calling his name will only encourage him on.

SEX LIFE

Sex does not usually play a very significant part in the life of a Border Terrier male. He is not often a nuisance in the home, mounting legs etc. Two males will sometimes mount each other, but this is mostly a dominance behaviour. If used at stud, some males will mark their territories indoors, as only dogs know how.

Bitches come into breeding condition (in season/on heat/in oestrus) twice a year, and care must be taken when exercising them for three weeks each time to prevent the unwanted attentions of the local dogs whose owners let them wander from home. A bitch is frequently a very willing partner in such liaisons, so be warned. Should a Border Terrier male be over-sexed, the remedy is castration, either by injection (chemical castration) or by a surgical operation. A bitch, once mature, can be spayed, but

When a Border Terrier is on a scent, he loses the ability to use his ears...

vomited; other times they pass through in a matter of minutes. Cleavers (goose-grass) is a special favourite, especially when young shoots appear. Some garden plants are poisonous, so I discourage my dogs from foraging there.

With more conventional foods, a Border Terrier is easy to please, but he does not seem to have the trigger that tells him he is full. If your dog wolfs up his dinner, do not be led to believe that he is still hungry. Give the appropriate amount and do not give in to those pleading eyes!

TRAINABILITY

Border Terriers seem unable to 'multi-task', rather like half the population! If the nose is being used, then the ears do not seem to work. Thus, if a Border Terrier is busy with his nose to the ground, it is a waste of time calling him until he raises his head. This may look like disobedience to the outsider – perhaps used to the instant reactions associated with a well-trained gundog – but it is something that we Border Terrier owners have grown to accept as normal behaviour. The Border Terrier has often been described as being quick to learn and slow to obey, but the breed is actually quite biddable within the limits of being a terrier.

House-training a Border Terrier puppy is started by his mother when she keeps her bed clean. The puppy follows her lead by leaving the bed to empty his bowels and bladder. The 'clean' area is extended over the first few

this can have side effects, such as increase in weight, softening of the coat and urinary incontinence.

FOOD ISSUES

Eating is an instinctive behaviour that all creatures possess; it is a necessary survival behaviour, and Border Terriers do not need any encouragement to display it! A delicate digestive system is a rarity in the breed: all manner of things are considered suitable to

the Border Terrier's palate if not to their owners. A Border Terrier will try anything – long-dead creatures, droppings from rabbits, sheep, cattle and horses, various plant materials, as well as non-organic matter such as stones, soil, socks etc. Most of what is consumed passes through the digestive system safely, but it is always wise to be vigilant with your Border Terrier. My dogs eat grass and grass roots almost daily. Sometimes these are quickly weeks of life to include as much of the house as possible, until the puppy is leaving the house to use whatever patch of grass is designated for this purpose.

Many puppies are clean by the time they go their new homes, but their bladders are not developed enough to last through the night. A Border Terrier puppy is usually very easy to house-train if the owner is vigilant and spots the signals from the puppy. The old-fashioned roll of newspaper administered to the puppy is cruel and unnecessary, and should only be used to chastise the owner for not taking more notice of the puppy's needs. For more information on house-training, see Chapter Four: The New Arrival.

GETTING ON WITH CHILDREN

Border Terriers seem to have an affinity with children; they must sense that these pack members are no threat to them but are vulnerable and need special attention. Or is it the sticky fingers and dropped food that attracts them? As with all dogs, children should be taught how to behave with a Border Terrier.

Puppies have little sharp teeth, which they use to explore the world, including little hands. I always tell children not to pull their hands away but to give a little yelp, just like a littermate would

when tackled too roughly. The puppy does not want to hurt anyone, and will be more careful next time.

A pack instinct I have observed with my Border Terriers occurs when one has injured himself and cries out in pain. The rest of the pack are there, instantly, ready to administer the coup de grace, if necessary. For this reason, I always supervise children and dogs playing together. Commonsense should tell everybody that a baby and a dog of any breed should never be left together unsupervised.

LIVING WITH OTHER DOGS/PETS

Border Terriers are naturally gregarious dogs and get on well

with other dogs, if properly socialised at the puppy stage. They can live amicably with the family cat, but care must be taken if there are pet rabbits or other small, furry creatures in the household. Border Terriers, like most terriers, cannot be trusted to leave these alone. You might be pleased with your terrier if he killed a rat, but he is not able to understand why you are cross when he kills the neighbour's guinea pig.

Border Terriers seem to have a natural affinity with horses and ponies, knowing how to avoid the hooves. Chickens and other feathered creatures are usually left alone, but, being a terrier, the Border's instincts can come to the fore.

If care is taken at the early stages, a Border Terrier will live happily with the family cat.

The Border Terrier is a natural worker and will thrive on being part of any hunting expeditions.

HUNTING, SHOOTING AND FISHING!

With their working ancestors never far behind any Border Terrier, it does not require much encouragement for a dog from more or less any strain to be trained for working purposes. There is not a division between working, show or companion Border Terriers – as there is, for instance, in some gundog breeds. Any terrier can be used for rabbiting or ratting, the Border Terrier included – and you will not be breaking any laws however many terriers are used.

Since the Hunting with Dogs Act 2004, we have to be more careful regarding traditional terrier work, as it is illegal to deliberately use a terrier to bolt a fox unless under special circumstances. For instance, a fox can be bolted using one terrier, but must be shot immediately; you need the written permission of the landowner, and the fox must be dispatched for the protection of game birds (not livestock such as sheep, or poultry). The law has yet to be tested in the courts regarding a dog which chases and kills a squirrel, but it would seem not to be illegal if you, the owner of the dog, had not *intended* the dog to chase and kill the squirrel.

DEER AND BOAR

In Scandinavia, the Border Terrier's highly developed sense of smell makes him an ideal dog for the specialised hunting of deer and boar. Hunters must have a licence to shoot, and one of the conditions of the licence is that there must be a dog used that is trained to follow a blood trail, such as left by a wounded quarry. In Sweden, Border Terriers are used to flush wild boar and foxes from cover for marksmen to shoot. In Denmark, Border Terriers do the same work, but on deer as well as the more traditional quarry, the fox.

FLUSHING GAME

In the UK, during organised 'shoots', where gundogs are used to flush game birds from cover for guns to shoot, the Border

Terrier has been found to be very useful in thick cover alongside the more traditional breeds, such as spaniels.

To do this work, the Border Terrier must be biddable, have courage and stamina, plus a thick coat to withstand brambles etc. One shoot, I have been told, regularly has five Border Terriers working, flushing game birds to the guns. They would not be tolerated on a shoot if they were not well behaved and did not do their job efficiently.

FISHING
Fishing? Yes, there is a Border Terrier in Denmark who accompanies his family on fishing trips and dives into the water to help land the fish!

ASSISTANCE DOGS
The special bond between man and dog has been developed for the benefit of people with disabilities in many ways. We have all heard of the wonderful work done by guide dogs for the blind over many years, but there are now other fields where the talents of dogs have been utilised. Border Terriers are not physically big enough to work as guide dogs or as disability assistance dogs, but they have proved themselves in other important spheres.

HEARING DOGS
The charity Hearing Dogs for Deaf People has been training dogs since 1982 to act as assistants and companions for people who are severely or profoundly deaf, and Border

A Hearing dog can transform the life of his deaf owner.

Terriers have been found to be ideal for this work. Hearing Dogs are chosen and trained for their friendliness and sociability. They are taught to respond to everyday sounds, like the doorbell, cooker timer or telephone, by touching their owner and leading them to the sound. The dog responds to emergency sounds, such as a smoke alarm, by touching his owner and lying down in a special alert signal.

There is a well-known Border Terrier called Baxter, who is very much an ambassador for Hearing Dogs. He goes with his owner to talks to promote the charity, and has even written a book about his exploits (with the help of his owner). Baxter was donated by his breeder to the charity, which trained him and then matched him up with his owner, who had asked for a dog who would share his hobby of walking. Baxter is but one Border Terrier who has found his niche in life – there are other Border Terriers, and a Border Terrier cross, who are also making an invaluable contribution to their owners' lives as hearing dogs.

Baxter shares a passion for walking with his owner Adam Wilson, and is also invaluable as an assistance dog.

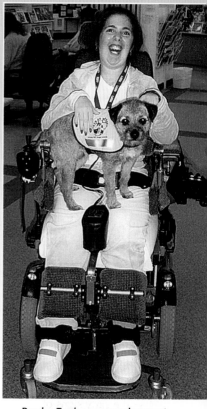

Border Terriers can make great therapy dogs.

THERAPY DOGS

Another field in which Border Terriers excel is as therapy dogs. The charity Pets As Therapy (PAT) has approximately 3,500 registered dogs visiting throughout the UK, and 78 are Border Terriers. The dogs and their owners visit people in hospitals, hospices, care homes, daycare centres, special needs schools and mainstream schools, enriching the lives of people unable to have a dog of their own.

Any dog can become a PAT (therapy) dog once he is over nine months old and has passed his assessment. The assessment will check that the Border Terrier is sociable and friendly without being over-boisterous. The dog must be calm and gentle when being groomed or stroked. He will also be tested to see how he reacts to sudden noises, such as a walking stick falling to the ground.

SEIZURE RESPONSE DOGS

Besides training disability assistance dogs, the charity Support Dogs also trains seizure response dogs, who alert their owners to an imminent epileptic seizure.

As with hearing dogs, the size of the dog is irrelevant, so Border Terriers are ideal for this

BRADY'S SPECIAL ROLE

The valuable and fulfilling work of a PAT dog is illustrated by Brady, a Border Terrier who visits hospitals. He is especially appreciated on the stroke rehabilitation ward. His owner gives the following account of his work:

"One lady had suffered a stroke and had not spoken since, until she saw Brady and said: 'Oh, dog.' It may not seem like very much, but it was a major achievement for her and a very emotional moment for her family (and me). We have noticed in several cases where a patient's speech has been affected that they may be embarrassed trying to talk in front of other people but will quite happily talk away to the dog, and this has been seen to stimulate long-term improvement.

"Another lady was due to go home, but, two days prior to her discharge, she suffered an extension to her stroke, which left her very ill and depressed. We visited her every day for a number of weeks and she told me that 'her little dog' was the only thing that kept her going. With this lady, Brady was exceptionally good and he would get on to the bed with her and fall asleep. He was so gentle and would not stand on her. This has been a constant source of pride and surprise to me – he is so intuitive and knows just when to be bouncy and friendly and when to be quiet and gentle."

work. Dogs cannot be trained to recognise the early signs of an epileptic seizure – it is an innate ability that only some display, but they can be trained to respond to a seizure. There is anecdotal evidence of Border Terriers who have an uncanny ability to communicate concern for their owner's health, so be aware if your Border Terrier is trying to tell you something.

AN IDEAL HOME

The Border Terrier is such an adaptable breed, there is no one ideal home to suit him. Border Terriers thrive under so many regimes. So, what makes a *non-ideal* home? A household where there is no one at home all day,

when the people leave for work and school in the morning and no one returns until late afternoon. This is not acceptable for any breed, and no one should place a puppy or adult in such a home.

Of course, work is a necessity nowadays, but it is possible to make provision for the needs of a dog by calling on the help of friends and neighbours, or professional dog sitters and walkers, to visit the home. Not ideal, but workable.

Border Terriers can live fulfilling lives in either town, village or country – it all depends on the attitude of the owners. Knowing the breed's background, you might think

that a country home would be ideal, but town and city dogs are often better catered for, with parks and opportunities for socialisation and training classes on hand. Dogs, including Border Terriers, cannot be allowed to run free in the country. We must respect the Country Code, so the right to roam is out of the question.

SECURITY ALERT

An ideal home usually includes a garden – definitely not an open-plan type garden – but one that is securely fenced in, for Border Terriers can squeeze through the narrowest of gaps if they decide this is what they want to do. Some can jump or climb fences,

Regardless of whether you live in the town or in the country, you must be on security alert, as Border Terriers are the escape artists of the dog world.

through the squares in the netting. Pig netting, which has smaller holes at the bottom of the fence, is not good enough either, as the Border Terrier soon discovers he can escape higher up the fence.

For my secure exercise paddock, I have used 3 feet (1 metre) sheep netting, with a barbed wire strand on top. This is covered with 5 feet (1.5 metres) of rabbit netting. The rabbit netting is buried 6 inches (15 cms) into the ground, and the top is angled in. It must look like a prison exercise yard, but it keeps the rabbits out and the Border Terriers in – apart from one dog who has developed a technique of hanging on top of the 5-foot (1.5-metre) gate and scrabbling over, using his hind legs.

FAMILY PACK

What is more important to a dog than his physical surroundings is his pack – his family. This might be one person or a whole tribe of adults and children. The Border Terrier likes nothing more than being with people, and if these people like doing the things he enjoys too, he is in heaven. He likes walking, new places to explore and new smells to savour. He will join in trips up mountains, strolls through forests, and splashing about on the beach. He will travel for miles in the car, taking up very little space, and will even be welcomed in hotels.

A Border Terrier is good company for anyone working

so you have to be one step ahead all the time. The jaws of a Border Terrier have tremendous strength and can tear through wire netting, so install heavy-duty wire at the beginning – don't wait until your dog has escaped.

Some owners train their dogs to stay within boundaries using an invisible fence, coupled with a radio-collar that the dog wears.

How effective this is with a Border Terrier, who is determined to chase a rabbit just outside the boundary, is debatable. The height of the garden fence is ideally 6 foot (2 metres)! This will deter all but the most determined jumper. Chain link is not ideal, as it can be climbed. Sheep netting is usually high enough, but most Border Terriers can easily get from home. He will sit next to you, perhaps leaning on your leg, not fussy or demanding attention, but giving you a good excuse to take a walk as a break from the computer. Any teenage boy who has countryside interests makes a good candidate for owning a Border Terrier puppy, provided he has the back-up of parents should his interests wander off in other directions. Retired couples, perhaps down-sizing their homes (and sometimes their dogs, too) also make ideal Border Terrier owners.

Outside normal family activities, there are many dog-orientated activities that the Border Terrier would enjoy. These include agility, flyball, terrier racing, junior handling, terrier shows, dancing with dogs, dog shows etc. Competitive obedience is not a Border Terrier's forte, but basic obedience is a must. All these activities are organised on a local level and can be accessed by looking for advertisements, going on-line and visiting appropriate websites, or asking at your local veterinary practice or pet shop.

In other words, a Border Terrier needs an active family to keep his mind and body healthy, and he will continue to give pleasure well into his teens.

The Border Terrier's dream is to have a varied and interesting life, in the company of his beloved human family.

THE FIRST BORDER TERRIERS

Chapter 2

W e know the Border Terrier today as a cheerful and friendly soul, much admired for his attractive looks. At present, Border Terriers are experiencing a huge increase in popularity, which is not always a good thing for a breed. In this chapter I would like to give some details on the Border's origins and development, which, perhaps, shows it in a rather different light and describes for the new owner the purposes and people behind this wonderful breed.

ORIGINS

The breed originates in the rough hill country centred around the Coquetdale region of Northumberland. The Border Terrier was bred purely to work to fox in this wild and difficult region. It is difficult in this day

and age of tarmac roads, motorised transport and complex technology to appreciate the terrain and conditions that gave rise to the Border that we know today – and the needs of the men who developed the breed. They required a tough and hardy little dog that could go anywhere with them, and do so day after day.

To try to put the development of the breed in context, I quote the comments below that were made by Vivian John Leahead Bucknall early in the 20th century. He was a great-nephew of Jake Robson senior and Jasper Dodd, and grandson of John Robson of North Tyne and Redewater – the men who, as you will see, were largely responsible for the development of the Border Terrier.

Fox-hunting was established in England in the 1700's. It seems that only the now comparatively rare

Smooth Fox and Wire-Haired Fox type terriers were used by the hunts of that time. A number of distinct pure-bred hunting terriers had not yet been recognised, such as the Black and Tan Terrier (whose club was founded in 1884), the Welsh Terrier (1886), the Lakeland Terrier, the Jack Russell Terrier, and the Border Terrier (recognised by the Kennel Club in 1920).

Few sporting country districts were without their own strain of 'working' terrier in which appearance was of minor importance so long as 'gameness' and 'stoutness' predominated.

There was, and is, no particular range or locality for these working terriers. They extended from the Scottish Border country in the North, to Devonshire in the West, and were to be met with in almost every intermediate county. In Devonshire, Parson John Russell, who was closely associated with the Devon and Somerset Stag Hounds in the late 1800s, possessed some almost entirely white, hard-jacketed little fellows whose good hunting qualities are now well known. Indeed, wherever hunting the fox or badger was followed, the latter and other good terriers were and are to be found. Such dogs vary in size but are usually less than 20lbs in weight, and, if well trained and entered, prove admirable hands at destroying vermin.

Trump: The Rev. John Russell's first terrier who was used to hunt fox.

One of the most useful strains of terrier is what was once described as the 'rough and ready' sort of dog kept in Northumberland and on the Borders region, which came to be known as the Border Terrier in the late 1800s – a name they take from their long association with the Border Hunt, a hunt which still exists, based at Otterburn in this district.

The Border Terrier acquired its name in about 1880, but the breed is not a modern creation. In the possession of the Robson family at Newton near Bellingham, there is a picture of a once well-known character in Tynedale, known as Yeddie Jackson, who was known as the hunter king in North Tyne throughout Liddesdale and the adjoining country. The painting, which was executed about 1820 or a few years later, included a Foxhound and a terrier, the latter being a good example of a Border.

Some of the terriers followed hounds and horses regularly, and were continually brought into use not only amongst the rocks and in rough ground of that kind, but in equally more dangerous places - wet drains or moss holes or waterfalls. A dog that goes in such a place may have to swim underground and find his fox, which is perhaps lying up in a side drain or earth. There are numerous crossings and cuttings in these peat moss drains, which may be natural or artificial. It is by no means unusual for terriers to become lost underground, and even when rescued to die later from the undue exertion, the lack of air, and the general unearthliness of being so many hours underground in a peat bog. The Border Terrier has an excellent constitution; if he had not, he would never have survived amongst the hardy northern sportsmen who considered him the best of all the working terriers.

A WORKING TERRIER

The Breed Standard, which is the blueprint describing the ideal Border Terrier, was heavily influenced by the views of the men who had developed the breed solely for the purpose of working it in the rough northern terrain. High on that list was Mr Jacob Robson of Byrness in Upper Redewater, who was Master of the Border Foxhounds for 54 years from 1879 to his death in 1933. He was followed by his son, who carried on the hounds with Mr Simon Dodd of Catcleugh until the death of the latter in 1951.

In describing what was required from the Border Terrier, 'Owld Jake' said – in about 1893:

"The strain of terriers that has been bred by my family, and in Northumberland and the Borders for so long, is now called the Border Terrier from the fact that they are principally used and bred in the extensive hill country hunted by the Border Foxhounds. The nomenclature is, however, of recent date, as they were used formerly to have no particular name, but were well known for their hardiness and gameness. Redewater, North Tyne, Coquet, Liddesdale and the Scottish Borders are the districts where they have been principally bred. My father, when he lived at Kielder, had some rare representatives of the breed, and Mr Hedley of Bewshaugh and Mr Sisterton of Yarrow Moor both near Falstone, North Tyne, have also bred excellent terriers of this strain. My father and the late Mr Dodd of Catcleugh preferred this breed of terrier to all others for bolting foxes, their keenness of nose and gameness, making them very

suitable for this purpose.

They vary in weight; 15lb to 18lb is their best size, as when bigger they cannot follow their fox underground so well, and a little terrier which is thoroughly game is always best. Flint, a mustard dog we had here nearly thirty years ago, was small but the best bolter of foxes I ever saw.

The favourite colour is red or mustard, although there are plenty of the variety pepper coloured, and others black and tan. Their coat or hair should be hard, wiry and close so as to enable them to withstand cold and wet. They have generally been bred for use and not for looks, but I have seen some very bonny terriers of this same strain. They should stand straight on their legs, with a short back, and not made like a Dandie Dinmont, long-backed and crooked; their ears ought to drop like those of a fox terrier, a strong jaw is a great point, but not nearly so long in the nose as the usual strains of Dandies and Scottish terriers. They may be either red or black nosed; in fact, the former colour is often preferred, as there is a belief that the red-nosed dogs are keener scented than those with black noses."

TERRIER BLOODLINES

It is said that the pure strains of Border Terrier, Dandie Dinmont and Bedlington Terrier all owe their origin to the impure strains of terriers owned by the tinkers in the Holystone and Thropton districts of Upper Coquetdale, Northumberland, in the 1700s and early 1800s. Yeddie Jackson has been mentioned, but another who was equally famous for his

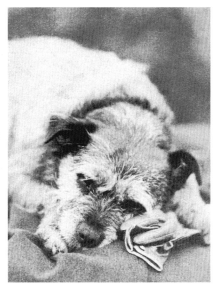

An early Border Terrier, c.1870.

hunting terriers at that time was Piper Allan, so nicknamed because he was a one-time piper to the then Duke of Northumberland.

At the start of the 20th century, most commentators agree that there were four types of terrier that had originated from common stock in the Border counties and these were used for killing foxes and other vermin. However, these types had become fairly well fixed for a considerable time before this; one is the Dandie Dinmont, another the Bedlington, leaving the other two distinct types in existence when the Border Terrier became a recognised breed under the Kennel Club.

It is generally agreed that, on registration, specimens of both types got on to the register. One of these is the terrier now

regarded as the right type of Border, which is the type that is so briefly but adequately described in the Breed Standard. The other was much shorter in the leg, longer and rougher in the coat (not a soft coat), and generally with a soft, light-coloured topknot like the Dandie and the Bedlington. This last type was believed to have existed chiefly on the east side and extended into Yorkshire and probably further south, and is often considered to be the origin of the present Norwich Terrier.

DEBATE AND CONTROVERSY

The Breed Standard, as finally agreed, is perhaps one of the briefest and least descriptive of those recognised by the Kennel Club, and should always be read in its entirety. The Standard was written by the men and women who had worked and known these terriers, over very many years, and they had a very clear idea of what they required.

However, even these brief requirements have given rise to an enormous amount of comment and debate over the years. Some examples of this are given below:

SIZE

The notes above contain the comments that: *"They vary in weight; 15lb to 18lb is their best size"*.

The original Standard drafted by the newly formed Border Terrier Club in 1920 stated:

BREED RECOGNITION

Moves towards Kennel Club recognition for the terrier so described were slow. Many of the breed's supporters did not agree with moving for recognition, feeling that the show bench was no place for a sporting dog and that many breeds were ruined by showing. Despite this, several attempts at recognition were made, starting late in the 19th century. These were not successful until a KC member, Captain Hamilton Adams, persuaded the KC that the Border Terrier was an old breed that was in the process of being revived. Recognition was granted and a Breed Standard was drawn up.

This Standard was not approved of by the breed's supporters, who consistently ignored it. However, in 1920 the Border Terrier Club itself was formed and drew up its own Standard, which members believed would protect the breed from ruination by the show ring. This Standard was accepted by the KC, and the first KC Standard was quietly dropped.

In 1921 the Northumberland Border Terrier Club was formed. It continued to oppose recognition, and was desirous of restricting membership to Northumberland – but with a grudging acceptance that people from the Borders could join! This club did not last long and, within a few years, its members had joined forces with the Border Terrier Club. A Standard was agreed upon, which was an amalgam of those proposed by both clubs. It remained virtually unchanged until 1986 when a standardization process by the KC resulted in a restructuring of all Breed Standards. However, the Border Terrier Standard remains almost identical to that drawn up by the breed club members.

"Size. Dogs should be between 14 & 17 lb in weight and 13 and 16 in. in height at shoulder. Bitches should not exceed 15 lb in weight and 15 in. in height at shoulder".

At about the same date, the short-lived Northumberland Border Terrier Club drew up its Standard, which stated: *"The Border Terrier should be a real Sporting Terrier, and not too large: Dogs 14 lb. Bitch 13 lb. Maximum."*

After a considerable amount of discussion, some of which became quite acrimonious, a compromise was reached, which tended to the lighter weights, and the final Standard, which is essentially the same today, states: *"Dogs 13 to 15¹/2 lbs, Bitches 11¹/2 to 14 lbs".*

It is not surprising, therefore, that the subject of size is one that has continuously exercised the breed with deep and ongoing concerns that dogs are becoming too big. Despite this, the majority of modern Champions could still come fairly close to the requirements if always on the heavier side.

PIGMENTATION

Jacob Robson comments that: *"They may be either red or black nosed; in fact, the former colour is often preferred, as there is a belief that the red-nosed dogs are keener scented than those with black noses."*

But the Standard states a preference for a black nose, although allows that a liver or flesh-coloured nose is not a serious fault. Breeders have certainly taken this clause to heart, for I have never seen a red or liver-coloured nose in the breed.

THE BODY

J.R. Carruthers, an early devotee of the breed, wrote of the Border: *"The neck should be moderately long and muscular and must not look short or thick; it should run into the shoulders with* no obvious thickening. The shoulder blades should be wedge shaped and close together at the top, that is, at the withers. If you can even put your finger between the blades at this point, there is something wrong. The shoulders should be well laid back: that is, they must have a good shape: A line drawn from the point of the shoulder to the withers should make an angle of at least 35 degrees with the vertical at the point of the shoulders no wider than the ribs.

The ribs should be well sprung but not round and the body should be rather long and deep but there should be no brisket below the height of the elbow.

I like a very slight arch above the quarters so as to give the hindquarters the essential racy look.

The front legs should be at the corners of the body, not set under it, and the dog must not be out at the elbows. The front legs should be close together and the chest must not be wide. You should not be able to put more than four fingers between the top of the legs - fingers differ in size but it must be less than a hand - four inches.

The thigh must be muscular and not rabbity. The hocks must be well let down as the dog should stand over a lot of ground for its size. The hind legs must be straight in line, neither close together nor spread out nor cow hocked.

The tail should not be too gay and in particular must not be curled over the back; it should be fairly short and thick at the root with a good taper. A thin or long tail is a definite fault.

The coat must be hard on the top with a good undercoat and the hide

Revenge: An early type of Border Terrier.
Walter Gardner's collection.

must be thick. So far as colour is concerned I have nothing to add to the official standard but I would like to emphasise that black is not blue. I have not seen a blue for a long time but those that were blue were the colour of a Bedlington or a Kerry Blue.

To my mind one of the best ways of judging the general appearance is a sideways view. The dog should in outline look like a well bred Hunter and not a Dales Cob. No terrier of any breed to my knowledge has the stamina of the Border; they can follow a horse all day after hounds."

Hugh Pybus (who started in Border Terriers at about the turn of the century and bred some of the early Champions), comments:

"When I was first brought into the breed (more than 60 years ago) I was told to judge the correct length of leg by putting my two hands one on top of the other under the brisket, this means at least eight inches ground clearance. We must at all costs avoid the Border Terrier suffering the same fate by, at any rate, three of the Scottish breeds which certainly now could not do the work they were originally intended for. Let it be remembered that in a hill country a fox seldom goes to ground in an earth like a south country fox but into a cleft in the rocks where the tunnel leading to the ultimate lying up place often crosses a fault or chasm which has to be jumped and the ultimate point is often on a shelf up to which a terrier has to fight his way."

When developing the breed along the lines that they required, the older breeders emphasised the necessity for narrow fronts and length of leg, features that distinguished them from most of the other types in the region. Whilst the Standard merely states that the body is "deep, narrow, fairly long", some older commentators were much more precise.

For example "...judge the correct length of leg by putting my two hands one on top of the other under the brisket, this means at least eight inches ground clearance."

I think that most modern breeders would be comfortable with this statement. I remember Mrs Bertha Sullivan, the greatest Border Terrier breeder of all time, stating that a dog should not be much above 13 inches at the withers, which roughly accords to this statement.

On the subject of width, Carruthers says: *"The front legs should be close together and the chest must not be wide. You should not be able to put more than four fingers between the top of the legs - fingers differ in size but it must be less than a hand - four inches."*

The Border is indeed a running dog and he does require some heart and lung room, but most modern breeders would dispute that you need quite this much!

THE HEAD

The great distinguishing feature of the breed is its head, and a great deal has been written on this subject over the years. The original Standard stated, "Head otter shaped, the skull should be flat and wide, the jaws, powerful and not pointed." The current Standard simply states that the head should be like that of an otter. Hugh Pybus, again writing early in the 1960s, has concerns about the developments then becoming apparent:

"I have for some time been taking such opportunities as have come my way to talk to some of the older breeders about heads; and all are perturbed at the recent trend to produce heads which are very different from those of Border Terriers at the time the standard was drawn up. The

The head is one of the most distinguishing features of the breed.

skull is tending to become coarse and there is over emphasis on a short foreface. The change is probably being brought about by judges and breeders who, either because they are not yet old enough, or for other reasons never had the opportunity of knowing the sort of terrier that was used by those who hunted at the time in question over the country of the Border between Scotland and England. It is thought that too much reliance has been placed on the wording of the standard, but no words can ever be devised for any standard to give a complete picture - the wording must be only a guide. Our object should be to maintain the breed as it was intended

to be by those who drew up the standard, with the characteristics they had in mind, and not to introduce what some people imagine to be an improvement. We do not advocate a long foreface nor a weak skull (particularly in dogs), but there should be moderation.

The head that is now being introduced has not, in many cases, the indescribable but definite Border characteristic. It will certainly produce whelping troubles. It is often nearly an apple head and the ears frequently are lying too much on the top of the head and it is generally accompanied by thickness at the shoulder."

Anne Roslin-Williams, a noted authority on the breed and one of the most successful of modern breeders, writes:

"What makes the true otter-head, rather than that presently acceptable 'border' head which we see so much? It is easier to say what it is NOT, rather then what it is. A broad (in moderation) almost flat skull, wide between the ears and with a good length from occiput to eye... The occiput is not obvious, being almost flat, but seen from above the skull finishes in a gentle curve behind the ears. In an otter the ears are set about two-thirds from the front of the skull, i.e. there is a considerable amount of skull behind the ears.

An apple-skull, where the skull is rounded, has a pronounced curve between the ears over the top of the skull and is quite incorrect although this is often mistaken for an otter-head. Correctly placed Border ears obviously enhance the appearance but it is possible to have incorrect ear carriage on a good skull as ear carriage is determined partly by muscular tension.

Otters have very little stop but are not absolutely flat between the eyes. There is a slight indentation like a thumb-print. A slight rising of the eyebrow pads enhance the otter-like appearance, as does a slight rising of the plane on each side of the skull between the eye and the ear.

Many Borders fall away here, although the centre of their skull might be quite good. I am talking about very slight mouldings on the head, not coarse lumps and bumps. The skull should feel one unit, which of course it is. In the best heads there are no deep crevices or lumps, on handling them.

The muzzle length is generally accepted to be about one third of the total length of the head, or slightly less. If it gets too short it looks incorrect and mouth troubles will follow, eventually. It must be filled under the eyes and continue filled right to the end of the muzzle, not falling away under the eyes like a pig and then coming out again to a well finished end, like a snout. The end of the muzzle can best be described as a rounded square, as if someone had sandpapered off the square corners.

Willie Barton's Border Terriers c. 1915. Walter Gardner's collection.

The mask ratios were dog 100:40, bitch 95:30 (length of skull:muzzle).

The nose bone must be straight, not in any way dished or tipped. The planes of the skull and muzzle are parallel and very nearly in a straight line, i.e. without a deep stop.

The Standard calls for a strong jaw. Many Borders have a decent top-jaw and appear to have a good head when viewed from above but fall away badly in under-jaw, lacking strength. This is probably where Border heads and Otter heads deviate most as otters have pinched bottom jaws by comparison. Their incisor teeth are tiny, being fish eaters, although their canines are large in comparison. Their incisors are very cramped and higgledy-piggledy as a result.
The Border must have big teeth and in a straight row or else they will be prone to damage. Hence he must have a broader jaw, and stronger, as he has to work against fox and is a meat eater.

The whole head must not be too

deep through, like a Bull breed. An Otter's head lies flat on the surface of the water barely noticeable, rather than sticking up like a floating box... Eye placement is important, but in my opinion eye shape (taken in context entirely of the otter-head, don't get me wrong and think I like it) if a bit too large and round need not necessarily detract from the otter-head. Otters have small round eyes."

However you describe it, the Border's head is its most distinguishing feature – and that expression of pure innocence, or total wickedness, is one of the most loveable and infuriating aspects of the breed.

COLOUR
Colour is another issue that has occupied the breed throughout its history. The early writers seem to have put very little emphasis on this point and were, more correctly, concerned about the quality of the coat and thickness of skin – vital issues for a working terrier whose life could depend upon them. In later years more attention was paid to trying to produce accurate descriptions of colour – the most contentious being the exact nature of blue and tan. Whatever, most modern commentators do agree that the colour originally described as

EARLY WINNERS IN THE SHOW RING

Teri: The first Champion in the breed.

Ch. Brimball Of Bridge Sollers: Winner of 15 CCs.

'wheaten' is no longer present in the breed, disappearing sometime in the mid-20th century. It is probable that this colour was genetically associated with a feature that breeders regarded as undesirable and so – inadvertently – discriminated against it until it eventually disappeared from the Border Terrier's genetic make-up.

EARLY WINNERS

By 1920 the breed was recognised and the Breed Standard agreed, and the way was now open for serious competition in the show ring. The stock that was considered good and typical all arose out of the Borders region, and originated from the dogs bred by the farmers and huntsmen in that region. The names of

Robson and Dodd, as well as many others, are deeply associated with the formation of the breed.

Two dogs were outstanding in producing the early winning stock, Titlington Jock and North Tyne Gyp. The first Champion was made in 1921; this was the dog Teri sired by North Tyne Gyp. Since records of the breed at this time were very scanty, most of the dogs in this pedigree were unregistered and many untraced – a situation made worse by the fact that so many had similar, and sometimes changed, names.

The first bitch to gain her title was Liddesdale Bess. She was owned by Mr Barton (another name closely associated with the breed), who described her as *"a grand little bitch, short coupled, dark red with a short thickset coat*

with hair like wire, she stood on her legs like a thoroughbred horse and had feet like a cat."

Two dogs, both owned by Adam Forster, are considered to be the keystones of the breed. These were Rival and Revenge, and virtually every modern Border can trace their pedigree back to some combination of the lines from these two dogs.

This is not the place to go into the detail of the breeding of all the early Champions, but, by the outbreak of war in 1939, the breed had made 55 Champions. The breed record was held by the bitch, Ch. Brimball of Bridge Sollers, with 15 Challenge Certificates. The highest registrations for the breed were in 1938 when 365 dogs were registered, taking the total over 300 for the first time. It is

INFLUENTIAL BORDER TERRIERS

Ch. Deerstone Falcliff Ramona: Considered by many to be the best example of a Border bred at the time (1967). Photo: Anne Roslin-Williams.

Ch. Irton First Footer: A prolific winner, he gained his Champion title in just two weeks, and went on to win nine CCs.

Ch. Dandyhow Cleopatra: She established the bitch record of 24 CCs. Photo: Anne Roslin-Williams.

Ch. Deerstone Destiny: An influential sire. Photo: Thurse.

Ch. Foxlair: He became a Champion in 1936.

Ch. Aldham Joker: This dog was made up just before the war, but had a big influence on post-war bloodlines.

difficult to judge these dogs from contemporary photographs, but most authorities agree that Ch. Foxlair – whelped in 1934 and made up in 1936 – is the closest to a 'modern' Border.

THE BORDER TERRIER IN AMERICA

The first Border Terrier was registered in the USA in 1927, although it is believed that a number had been imported prior to that. Throughout the 30s a few more were exported from the UK, but it was not until a bitch in whelp to the great Ch. Foxlair was imported that the first American Champion was made in 1941.

In the early days of the breed in the USA, two kennels were very influential: William MacBain's Diehard kennel and Dr Merritt Pope's Philibeg kennel. Am. Ch. Diehard Dandy and Dr Pope's Am. Ch. Philibeg Red Miss were the first male and female American-bred Champions.

Marjory Van der Veer and Margery Harvey obtained the foundation of their Dalquest kennel, Am. Ch. Philabeg Red Bet, from Merritt Pope in 1947. They imported several Portholmes, including Ch. & Am. Ch. Portholme Macsleap, and went on to produce 44

Ch. & American Ch. Portholme Macsleap.

Ch. & American Ch. Workmore Waggoner.
Photo: Anne Roslin-Williams.

AMERICAN BREED CLUBS

The Border Terrier Club of America did not come into existence until 1949 with 10 members, including Dr and Mrs Merritt Pope, William MacBain and the Dalquest ladies. Marjory Van der Veer was secretary of the BTCA for 32 years.

The BTCA currently has almost 800 members with about the same number of registrations per annum. The first Specialty was held in 1959; in 1986, two Specialties were held. From the 1970s onwards, eight regional breed clubs gradually came into being, running their own events, including Specialties. The BTCA Specialty is now known as the National Specialty.

Champions as well as providing important foundation stock for several other kennels.

The Dalquest kennel was, for many decades, a keystone of the breed in the USA. It was joined from the 1950s onwards by Kate Webb's Shelburne kennel and Marion DuPont Scott's kennel (which, in accordance with old Border tradition, did not have an affix). Good stock was imported from the UK and the breed steadily made progress.

While the American Border was firmly based on UK imports,

changes in the recent changes in regulations, which allow for much greater freedom of movement, mean that breeders can now access the Border gene pool worldwide – offering exciting opportunities for breeding in the future.

CURRENT STATUS

For much of its history, the Border Terrier has been something of a specialist's dog and it remained very strong and popular in its heartlands in the north of England and the

Borders. It slowly spread worldwide, being particularly popular in the Scandinavian countries. Always a breed for the terrier enthusiast, the Border Terrier has now established itself as a favourite among pet owners with registrations increasing at a rapid rate. It is now firmly established in the top ten of the UK's most popular breeds.

It is difficult to know what to ascribe this meteoric rise in popularity to. Certainly, it is a trouble-free, healthy, adaptable little terrier – a no-nonsense, sensible little dog with no inbuilt health problems. Maybe this started the landslide, coupled by the increasing success of the breed in the show ring. Up until this time most breeders were interested in the breed either as show dogs or workers; they were a knowledgeable group who had a deep and abiding interest in these wonderful little dogs.

Unfortunately, the increase in popularity was not always to the breed's benefit, with commercial gain taking priority over the health and welfare of the breed. Thankfully, there is still a significant body of dedicated enthusiasts with great affection for, and great knowledge of, the breed who will safeguard the future of this small but great-hearted little terrier.

Despite growing numbers, breeders are striving to preserve the very best of this remarkable breed. Photo: Tracy Morgan.

A BORDER TERRIER FOR YOUR LIFESTYLE

Chapter 3

As secretary of The Border Terrier Club, I am often contacted by people who have decided they would like to own a dog and are thinking about buying a Border Terrier. Many of these have been in full-time employment and have waited for a change in lifestyle, such as retiring or working part-time, before fulfilling their lifelong ambition to own a dog.

However, sadly, some of those who contact me do not have such plans. They intend to be out of the house for 10 hours or more a day, but see nothing wrong in expecting a dog to be content left alone for that length of time. It is all too easy to decide you want a dog, but to forget about the time it takes to house train a puppy, or to help an older rescued dog to readjust to a new home environment with new people and rules. I relate to them details

of families who have called me up when everything is going wrong: their energetic Border, left alone all day, is barking continuously and annoying the neighbours; or they are coming back to find the dog has messed in the house and/or chewed off the wallpaper or other household items.

In my view, all these things are the fault of the owner and are never the fault of the dog, and my sympathies here are with the poor Border. If people would only consider if it is the right thing to do *for the dog*, before rushing out to buy one, there would be far fewer dogs in rescue.

It is, of course, possible to have a happy, healthy, well-adjusted and well-exercised dog while working full-time, but you cannot expect to leave any dog unattended all day. Arrangements have to be made for the dog to be given some exercise, a chance to relieve himself at regular

intervals, and to have a break from the house during the day. If you are going out for a morning, take your Border Terrier on a long walk before you leave, so that he has had his breakfast, had a walk and some play time, and will be happy to sleep for a few hours before the lunchtime walker arrives. If you know that you cannot do this, then it is best not to purchase a dog, but to wait until your lifestyle and work schedules are such that it is the right time. You cannot put a dog away after a couple of weeks if you tire of it. It is a long-term commitment.

HOLIDAYS

Since we purchased our first Border Terrier, we have not taken any holidays, apart from those where we took the dogs with us, or where our daughter has stayed in our house as dog sitter for a few days. There are many dog-

Think long and hard before you take on the commitment of owning a Border Terrier.

friendly places to stay in the UK. It is important that if you take your dog on holiday with you, that you have a second disc made for his collar with your contact details at the holiday destination.

If you like to go abroad on holiday and are not taking your dog with you, then you need to find a good boarding kennels. I would recommend visiting a few boarding kennels before you decide which one to use. If you have any doubts about a particular

kennel, then do not leave your dog there. There are also dog sitters who will look after your dog in your own home, or in a private home. Before you decide which to use, consider the safety and security of your pet above all else. Boarding kennels should have full insurance, and should also have two doors between your dog and the outside world, to ensure he cannot slip past someone and escape. In a private home, you will not have this knowledge of security.

FINANCE
Dogs cost money! Not such a surprise, I know, but you need to factor into your list of expenses the cost of food, bedding, toys and treats, and also veterinary costs. When selecting a veterinary practice, you will be more concerned with the quality of the care from the vet and his/her staff than with the cost, but it may be worth checking out the cost of routine injections etc. before choosing which vet to use.

Rain, shine, or snow, a Border Terrier needs daily exercise.

You may also consider taking out pet insurance, so that in the event of your dog being ill, or in an accident, you will have the vast majority of your vet's bills paid for you. Shop around for the right insurance; there are many more firms providing pet insurance, so read the small print carefully before you sign up. Some firms only insure dogs until a certain age, and with most companies you will pay the first £50 or so of any treatment.

It may be best to look for a lifetime plan where there will be no upper age limit, and, if the dog develops a chronic condition, payment lasts the length of the condition and not just the first 12 months. Pre-existing conditions are usually not provided for under insurance, so it is best to take out insurance at the start of your pet ownership rather than waiting until something goes wrong.

If you groom your Border yourself, then the cost of purchase of the necessary equipment may be minimal (see Chapter Four), or you may push the boat out a little more and buy a grooming table. If you feel you really are unable to groom a Border (and it is not difficult with a little practice), then consider taking your dog to a grooming parlour to be hand-stripped. This usually costs more than clipping, as it takes longer.

BORDER TERRIER

MALE OR FEMALE?

Border Terrier males can be as placid and loving as the females, and sometimes the females can be more feisty than the males – it all depends on each individual dog or bitch, how they are raised and how you train them. So if the right breeder for you has one puppy available and it is a dog, but you were thinking of getting a bitch, do not discount a good, sound, loving, well-reared puppy. Discuss your concerns and ideas with the breeder, and have a look at the puppy before you decide.

COLOURS

There are four colours in the Breed Standard, but, in reality, you will probably be choosing between grizzle and tan, and blue and tan, as red Border Terriers are few, and a true wheaten colour has not been seen in the breed for 30 years or more.

Sometimes the puppy will have some white on the chest. A small amount is acceptable in the breed. In a very young puppy, the amount can seem quite large but usually diminishes as the puppy grows. There should not be any white anywhere else on the body, although sometimes there are a few white hairs on the tips of the paws, which come out when the dog is groomed. Beware, though, of any 'Border Terrier' with a full white paw or two – this is never seen in a pedigree Border and you would probably need to check if there were any other breeds of dog on the premises that could be the guilty party!

When the Border's coat grows, the dead hairs generally become lighter. These will come out when you strip the dog. In addition, there is a band of different-coloured hair towards the base of the tail, which is located around a scent gland and is a feature of this and other breeds and not to be worried about!

MORE THAN ONE?

There is a danger that you will think at the outset that two dogs may be better than one, and there are some breeders who may even try to convince you to buy two puppies from their litter when you only wanted one. If that is the case, run! Any knowledgeable breeder, who cares about their puppies, will not allow you to take more than one puppy, and should certainly never suggest it to you. Puppies of the same age may get along nicely for a while, or even forever, but there is a strong possibility that, at some stage, you will have problems with them. They may become too focused on each other, or they may become argumentative – and that can turn nasty very quickly.

A male Border Terrier (right) can be as affectionate as a female (left) – it all comes down to the individual.

I frequently receive calls from upset owners whose little sweet darlings have turned into raging furies, in front of their eyes, when they did not see anything leading up to it. There were probably some body language signs, which the owners did not recognise, some stiffening of the body and a turn of the head, before the dogs launched into a full-blown fight, but even the most experienced of terrier owners can get a shock when two puppies or older dogs exchange one glance, start to fight and thereafter become lifelong enemies. Border Terriers latch on to each other if they decide to fight, and it can be very difficult to break them up. This can even happen with puppies as young as 14 weeks, with both dogs and owners getting badly bitten.

Once two Border Terriers have had a serious fight, there is a greater risk of future conflict – some may not even be able to be in the same room without starting up straight away. You may think you can get around this, and try to keep the situation under review. But sooner or later, it is probably best to realise that one of the dogs has to be rehomed for the sake of peace and quiet in the home, and in your best interests and those of your dogs!

If you want two Border Terriers, wait at least a couple of years before considering bringing another dog into your home. It is more likely for same-sex couples to fight (but not unknown for opposite sexes), so it is best if your second Border is the

BORDER TERRIER COLOURS

You will probably choose between a blue and tan (left) and a grizzle and tan (right). The blue and tan's coat appears black to begin with.

A blue and tan (left) and a grizzle and tan (right) showing their adult colours.

Border Terriers are not argumentative dogs and enjoy each other's company.

opposite sex to the one you already have. Then, of course, you need to consider having the male castrated or the female spayed, unless you want mayhem twice a year for three or more weeks at a time. I once had someone ring me who had mother and son which they had kept together; they were so surprised when son mated mother, thinking they would not do that! They can and they will, and it is up to you to ensure that it does not happen!

COMPANION DOGS

If you wish your dog to be primarily a companion for you and your family, you may be more concerned about the temperament of the puppies, their parents and previous generations than with the Breed Standard. However, it would not harm you to read the Breed Standard before going to see the puppies, not least to be aware that this is a working terrier breed

and should be very energetic and lively (for 'lively' sometimes read 'trouble'!). It is no good expecting your puppy to sit like a little dog of wood. He will have his quiet moments for sure, but he is not a Toy breed and you may anticipate a greater level of activity from him than from some types of dog.

SHOW DOGS

If you would like to show your Border Terrier, then it may be best, before choosing your breeder, to attend some shows and see if any line of dogs in particular attracts you. Have a chat with their breeder and see if they are producing a litter in the near future. You may have to wait a while for the right puppy from your breeder of choice, but it will be worth it in the long run.

All our dogs are house pets first and show dogs second. The time they spend with you in the show ring is a very small part of their

time with you as companions, and you may be keeping the puppy as a pet, if he does not make it as a show dog. Sometimes a breeder will run a puppy on to see if it will make the grade as a show dog, but it does not always fulfil its early promise.

Beware of adverts stating "ideal for work, show or pet". No breeder can guarantee that a puppy will make it into the show ring. The most they can say is that it has promise. The breeder should advise you what they see as the best points and the not-so-good points of that particular puppy as compared to the Breed Standard. The ideal dog has never been born, so beware of exaggerated claims of grandness!

If you have ambitions to show your Border Terrier, you will need to make a special evaluation of a puppy's conformation, as well as assessing his temperament. When we are looking for a puppy to show from our breeding, we look to the Breed Standard (see Chapter Seven) to see how closely the puppy compares to it.

THE HEAD

The head is a very important part of this breed. You could have the best Border Terrier in the world, with a lovely body, but if he has an untypical head, then he is just another terrier. So we look for a puppy with a short, strong muzzle, with proportions of one-third from nose to stop and two-thirds from stop to occiput (the top of the head), with not much stop, but with a smooth flow-through like that of an otter. You can get the idea of the 'look' of an otter, by moving the dog's ears out of the way with your hand and looking at the head from the side.

When a puppy starts to teethe, he may hold his ears awkwardly, flying away from the side of the cheek. But when he is an adult, his ears should drop forward close to the cheek and not break above the level of the top of the head. Some Borders continue to fly their ears as adults, and this is most frustrating when you are showing them. If you have done your homework, you should know whether both parents had good heads, which might or might not mean the puppy stands a chance of having a good otter head. In any litter, there will be some with better heads than others. We were once told that when you see a bad head at eight weeks, with, say, a narrow, weak muzzle, it will never become a good head. Conversely, what looks like a good head at eight weeks can change to a poor head by the time the dog matures. So nothing is set in stone. You pays your money and you takes your choice!

There is no guarantee that a puppy will become a top winner in the ring – all you can do is assess show potential.

The correct scissor bite, with top teeth closing overlapping the bottom teeth, is very important, as undershot or overshot mouths are a major fault and highly undesirable. Such a Border should not be shown or bred from. However, at eight weeks, your Border has only his puppy teeth, which may be correct. The important stage is at four to five months when he starts to change to his adult teeth. Many a breeder has had an upset at this stage, where a very promising puppy has changed his teeth and become undershot. So, check the puppies' teeth at eight weeks by all means, but do not blame the breeder if the mouth is not right by six months. This is a shame, but there is nothing to be done about it and you have to say "that's life" and move on.

MOVEMENT
Movement is very important in the breed. The Border is essentially a working terrier, so he should have no exaggerations. He should be capable of doing a day's work, following the horses when out with the hunt, but still able to go to ground at the end of a long day. We pay particular notice to a puppy's bone structure, ensuring the forelegs are straight and not too heavy in bone. We also look for the

The Border Terrier must have a typical 'otter' head, and this should be apparent from an early age.

correct movement. While an eight-week-old puppy may be a little loose in front movement, which you may forgive at this stage as he's still a baby, you would not want any flipping movement of the front paws, or any cow hocks in the rear. Move the puppy up and down and watch the movement carefully.

You also need to check the angulation of the shoulder. If the puppy has incorrect shoulder placement, it may mean he lifts his legs up too high when moving, rather like a prancing horse. Also check the length of the neck, which should give the puppy an overall balanced

appearance, so that all is in proportion.

RIBCAGE
The shape of the ribcage is very important in a working terrier, as he should have the ability to go to ground after a fox. Running your hands along the dog, thumb on one side of the body and the rest of hand on the other side, feel the shape of the rib. In a litter of puppies, you can compare and contrast the rib shape one to the other and discount the puppy who has a barrel-shaped rib. The rib should not be flat, but there should be a slight change in the shape as you move your hand along, and the ribs should be carried well back.

TOPLINE AND TAILSET
Look for a level topline, and for a tail that is not low set nor so high that it is carried over the back. The tail should be thick at the base and tapering, and has been likened to a carrot shape. A long thin tail, waving around right over the back, is not correct and unbalances the dog to the eye.

FEET, COAT AND SKIN
The correct feet, coat and skin enable the dog to do his job

without getting injured. Feet should be small with thick pads, while the correct double coat, with harsh topcoat and thick undercoat, assist the dog when he is out in all weathers. His skin should be supple and thick, so he can squiggle around underground and not be torn to shreds by the fox in any close encounter.

TESTICLES

With a male puppy, you are looking for two testicles fully descended into the scrotum. Sometimes they are not fully descended at eight weeks. However, if your Border has reached six months and has only one, or none, then you may wait until 12 months to be sure, but it looks as if you will be disappointed. You should then consult a vet, as undescended testicles increase the risk of cancer and the dog will probably need to be castrated, as he should not be bred from, nor shown.

If you are purchasing a Border with a view to showing him, to avoid disappointment in this area, if would be best if you could feel, or at least see, both testicles fully descended into the scrotum at eight weeks old. If not, with a seven per cent incidence of one or both failing to drop in this breed, then you may feel it is not worth taking a gamble, if showing is a very important reason why you are purchasing this puppy. If the worst happens and you decide to rehome your puppy as you

The breeder will 'stand up' a puppy to help you to assess his conformation.

cannot show him, then you will tell the new owners that it is likely they should have the dog castrated in the future to avoid the risk of testicular cancer in later life. If in doubt, consult a vet, who will advise the best way forward.

MODERATE/MODERATELY/ MODERATION

These words in the Breed Standard are very important; apply them when you are looking at your prospective show puppy, as the Standard says: "Moderately broad in skull", ears "of moderate thickness", neck "of moderate length" and tail "moderately short".

IN ESSENCE

I also apply the above words of moderate and moderation to the

whole dog, looking for an unexaggerated, free-moving, agile dog. In essence, this is a working terrier, which should be able to do a job of work, and moderation with no exaggerations should assist that.

Read the Breed Standard over and over again before you go to select your puppy. If this is your first show dog, take someone along with you, with the breeder's permission, to help you make your choice. A good breeder, who knows the breed well, should also point out to you both the good and bad points of all the puppies and guide you to the right one. Remember: there was never a perfect dog born, so decide what appeals to you, and hopefully your instinct will help you choose!

FINDING A BREEDER

Never buy a Border Terrier on a whim, ringing a number after casually glancing through the paper and happening upon adverts of dogs for sale. Never purchase a dog from anyone other than the breeder, unless you are rescuing an older dog. If you are looking for a puppy, contact the Kennel Club (see Appendices) for details of breeders who have puppies available. These are not 'recommended' by the Kennel Club, as some people seem to believe, but are breeders who have registered their litters with the Kennel Club and paid an additional fee to have their puppies included in a list. The Kennel Club can also supply you with a list of Accredited Breeders, who promise the Kennel Club they will abide by an expected standard of care with regard to breeding and sale of their puppies. Details of the Accredited Breeder Scheme can be viewed on the Kennel Club website.

You can also obtain the number of your local breed club secretary, who may be able to help you find a breeder who is a member of their club. Each club has its own code of ethics and its members agree to abide by that code. It is helpful if you obtain a copy of the code of ethics for that club, to check that the breeder is abiding by them and to see what standards of care you should be looking for in a breeder.

VISITING A BREEDER

When you first visit a breeder, you will want to see the mother of your puppy and any other family members who live with the breeder. Unless the dam has died, never purchase a puppy without first having seen his mother.

You may visit the breeder before the puppies are born, but if they are already born when you contact the breeder, it is wise to wait until the puppies are at least four weeks old, arranging a date and time suitable to the breeder. You should not visit the puppies if you have another dog at home that is ill, or if you have come into contact with such a dog, as you could bring a virus to the unvaccinated puppies, which may prove fatal to them.

Some breeders, myself included, like to meet the

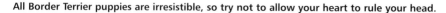

All Border Terrier puppies are irresistible, so try not to allow your heart to rule your head.

prospective owners a few times before they take the puppy at around eight weeks old or more, so there is plenty of time to talk about the puppies and the breed, and for both sides to get to know each other and ask plenty of questions. If I am not sure that the person is right for this puppy, then they will not be allowed to have him. Similarly, if you, as the prospective owner, have doubts, it is best not to proceed.

The breeder will tell you all the best and worst things about owning a terrier – and a Border in particular – and will check your suitability as a prospective owner of this breed. Judge the breeder by the amount of questions they ask you about your ability to look after their precious puppy. If the breeder is happy to let you have a puppy and asks for a deposit before meeting you, or before discussing your lifestyle and how the dog or puppy will fit in, then you may have to rethink whether this breeder really cares about the breed and the welfare of their puppies, or if they are only breeding for money.

The amount of help and guidance you get before you take your puppy may be an indication of the amount you will get after you have bought the pup. If you are asked so many questions that you start to feel a little insulted, then that, to my mind, is a caring, responsible breeder, but when a decision is reached by both sides, there should be a level of trust between breeder and puppy buyer.

Similarly, if you are taking on an older dog, or one from a Border Terrier rescue scheme, you should expect a lot of questions to ascertain if you are the right person for that particular dog. You should also be given a lot of advice on how to care for the dog, with full details of any difficulties the dog is having, so you can address those issues with care and concern for the dog's welfare.

HEALTH CHECKS

Some breeders will obtain a health certificate from their vet, which will include a general check of ears (to ensure no ear mites), eyes (to check if there is any indication of a health problem), skin (to ensure no parasites), heart (to ensure no heart murmur) and general body

Puppies do sleep a lot, so you will need to find a time when they are lively and active before making your choice.

LOOKING FOR A PUPPY OR ADULT DOG TO JOIN YOUR HOME?

10 GOLDEN RULES

1. Research the breed of your choice; what are its good and bad points? Beware of a breeder who only tells you the good points about the breed; are they more interested in the money than your choice of breed being right for you? Try to see the breed at, perhaps, a dog show where there will be a few entered – perhaps a breed club show, where you can talk to breeders and exhibitors and learn a little more about the breed. Buy some books on the breed, or ask your library to stock some. Talk to breed club secretaries and visit club websites, where there will be lots of information about your chosen breed. Some general websites give misleading information about some breeds, so beware of where your research takes you. For example, some websites say that certain breeds of dog are good for asthmatics, when that is not the case, so always check this out with a reputable source.

2. Always see the puppies with their mother (you may not always be able to see the father, as the breeder may have chosen a dog who lives many miles away, but you should always see the puppies with their mother).

3. Ensure that the puppy is at least seven weeks of age, or preferably eight weeks, when you go to pick it up. On no account should a puppy go before it has reached seven weeks of age.

4. Ensure the puppies have been socialised by the breeder – handled and played with (not just left in a shed or barn with no interaction with humans). Puppies starved of human contact may be more difficult to bring into a household situation and may be frightened of humans and resistant to handling.

5. Make sure the puppies do not have parasites, such as ear mites, worms or fleas. The breeder should have wormed the puppies at least three times before they leave their premises. The breeder should tell you what worming preparation they used and the dates they used them.

6. Always take the puppy to your chosen veterinary surgery shortly after purchase, so they can perform a health check. The breeder may have obtained a health certificate from their own vet before you buy the puppy, which they will give to you. Vets usually check such things as ears, skin condition, heart (for heart murmurs) and eyes. This will only be a general health check, but is a better than nothing. Some breeds suffer from hereditary conditions (such as hip dysplasia, cataracts, fits etc); you should research whether your chosen breed is regularly screened for certain conditions. Concerned breeders will have had all the necessary health checks done for their breed, checking out both parents before they use them, and will be able to show you the documentation. For more information on health checks, see Chapter Eight: Happy and Healthy.

7. The breeder should tell you what brand of dog food (or what feeding regime they have been using) for the puppies. They may give you a small supply of the food to take with you. At eight weeks, most breeders will be feeding the puppies about three or four times a day. You should be prepared to do the same. Do not change the type of food, as this may cause the puppy to have an upset tummy. Stick with what the breeder has been using and if, at a later date, you do decide to change, do this gradually over a period of about a week, introducing a small amount of the new food mixed with the regular food and then 50/50 then later 75/25 and eventually, all new food. Then keep using that food. Chopping and changing food regularly can upset the digestive system of your puppy.

8. Be prepared for a large change in your household routine, as house training a puppy is not always easy and he or she will make many mistakes. But remember, all the mistakes a puppy makes are your fault, not the puppy's fault. He or she is just a baby and needs time to learn. Be kind and consistent. Be prepared to leap about for a few weeks, looking for the signs that the puppy wants to go and then taking him outside and praising him

when he does it in the right place. Never scold the puppy for the accidents. They are your fault, as you have not recognised the signs in time.

9. When you leave the puppy alone, do so for short periods of time to start with, so he learns that you go away – but that you come back. If you take some time off work to look after the new arrival, do not make the mistake of staying with him 24 hours a day for two weeks and then going to work and leaving him alone for eight hours. He may develop separation anxiety and howl and cry all the time you are gone. Instead, bring him home, play with him, feed him, make sure he has been to the toilet and that he is tired and then pop him in his bed in a safe place and leave him alone for a couple of hours. Go into another room, go out shopping, anything, just leave him alone, so he learns that there will be times when he is on his own. You could leave a radio on playing quietly and perhaps some toys (but these should be safe ones that he cannot tear up and choke on).

10. Ensure that you have the time and space to devote to a puppy and can give him a permanent, loving home, with sufficient food, warmth and exercise. Every member of the family should want the puppy, but if any of your family has reservations about having a dog in the household, this will impact on the dog's happiness and well-being in the future.

(Compiled by Anne Gregory of the Scottish Border Terrier Club and Kathy Wilkinson of The Border Terrier Club, in conjunction with other Border Terrier Clubs in the UK.)

If you are taking on an older dog, check out his health record and find out as much information about his background as possible.

any preparations needed. Some people do not believe in using flea treatments if there are no signs of fleas, as they feel this is putting chemicals on to a dog when there is no need. Your vet can also undertake an early check on your puppy and advise you if he is free from parasites.

You should ensure the puppies are lively (unless they have just gone to sleep after a meal and a play, in which case you should visit again at a later date). Baby puppies do spend a lot of time sleeping. We once had an extremely lively litter of puppies, but every time one particular family came to visit, no matter how I tried to time the puppies' feed and play time to ensure they were awake, they always managed to race about wildly playing and then fall asleep just as the couple's car drove up to the house! It took three visits before they saw the whirling dervishes that they really were and not the lovely sleepy babies in the nest!

Your general check of the puppy at the breeder's premises should also include looking at their eyes and nose to ensure there are no discharges, and a check on their body to ensure they are nicely covered and not thin, but neither pot-bellied (as that can indicate a heavy worm burden). Always ask when the puppies were wormed and what with, so you know when you should next worm your puppy. We always use wormers from the vet rather than any available in a pet shop. You want to be sure the wormer will not hurt the

condition and weight.

When you visit the breeder's premises and look at the puppies, you should ensure they have no parasites, such as fleas, by checking them over when you are playing with them. Also check that there is no discharge from the eyes and ensure that the ears are clean and free from discharge

or strong smell, which could indicate ear mites or canker. It would not be good to notice fleas on your puppy on the journey home! Ask the breeder if any flea treatments have been used and, if so, when and what was used. Armed with this information to pass on to your vet, you can follow your vet's advice regarding puppy, so follow the vet's guidelines as to amount and times precisely.

Check that there are no signs of diarrhoea or sickness. If you are in any doubt, ask that the puppy sees a vet and has a health certificate before you take him home. If the puppy is ill in any way, it is best if he recovers at the breeder's before you take him home and compromise his system further with the stress of moving home. Many puppies may have loose stools in the days following a home move, with a change of environment and people, so it is important that they start out as healthy as possible and that you take your puppy to your own vet for a health check within a day or two of bringing him home. If your puppy becomes ill after you get

him home, take him to your vet immediately.

HELPLINE

If you have any questions about the breed or about your puppy, firstly go back to your breeder. If they care about their puppies, they will have kept in touch with you and they will be more than willing to help you address any concerns you may have now or at any time in the future.

Before you take your puppy home, it might be as well to ask if you can come back and be shown how to strip the puppy when he is ready, and if you can ring them if you have any concerns. The breeder may ask you to sign an agreement that you will return the puppy to them if at any time in the future you are unable to care for him –

or at least advise them, so they can help you find another home, rather than allowing the puppy to be passed from one unsuitable home to the next.

If you have doubts about your ability to spend the time needed to help the puppy grow into a happy, healthy, well-loved Border Terrier, then reconsider not only for your own sake – but most importantly, for the puppy's sake.

LAST THOUGHTS

As I have said before: never buy a dog on a whim. Your Border may require a lot of your time and energy to make his life and yours a happy partnership, but if you take all that time and you put in all that effort, you will both reap the rewards. Best of luck for a long and happy life together!

Taking on a Border Terrier is a big step but if you work hard at his care and training, you will be richly rewarded with a wonderful companion.

THE NEW ARRIVAL

Chapter 4

I f you have not had a dog before, then some of the things you need to check prior to his arrival may seem obvious, or perhaps you had just not thought of them, so here goes! Even if you have had a dog before, the one you are about to take into your home now will not have a sign on his head saying 'chewer', so do not let a previous 'goody two shoes' lull you into a false sense of security!

DOG-PROOFING YOUR HOME

In the rooms to which your dog will have access, such as the lounge, dining room or kitchen (and, for some, the bedrooms), you need to make an initial check of anything that may harm the puppy or older dog, and anything of value that he may harm for you!

Electricity can be very

CHEWING CHECKLIST

I have known people who have had the following items chewed (some, sad to say, were ours): remote controls (for the television, video, CD player, etc), mobile telephones, wallet and money, shoes, children's toys, wallpaper, wall, three-piece suite, corner of kitchen units, slippers, socks, thongs (one item not needed in this household), and so on – the list is endless...

The message is to be vigilant, and please do not blame the dog if you find something chewed up, as it will be your fault for not making sure that the items were placed out of harm's way, or that the puppy or dog was put somewhere where they could not get into mischief.

Young puppies chew when they are teething and sometimes grow out of it. Bored dogs of any age cannot read the newspaper, watch the television or read a book, but they can and do wee, poo and chew!

A Border Terrier is lively and inquisitive and so you need to make sure your home is 100 per cent safe.

dangerous, both for a young child and a puppy or older dog. Check in the rooms for any loose wiring or leads from electrical equipment or telephones, and ensure these cannot be chewed should your attention be elsewhere for more than a minute. Not only may he harm himself, but also a chewed wire can be a fire hazard – so be safe.

Next, have a look around the room and see which furniture you are fond of, as that may be the target for small teeth. Puppies that are teething are particularly

fond of gnawing things, but some dogs never grow out of the chewing stage; they're just hiding it from you until that time when you leave them alone with your best settee for company!

If you are leaving your puppy or dog alone for some time, try to make sure he is tired. Play with him and take him for walks to burn off his excess energy, and then put him into a room where he cannot damage anything. It might be wise, when he is young, to confine him to a crate when you are out, but you should only

do so once he has eaten, had a chance to play, and had the opportunity to 'toilet'.

A Border should not be left in his crate for more than a few hours, and he should have access to water at all times, especially if you are feeding him dry food. The water should be accessible, but not able to be tipped over. We use a bowl that drops into a wire holder, hooked on to the inside of the cage, but we also tie the holder on to the cage with plastic tapes, which he cannot reach.

Check out the garden and make sure that it is escape-proof.

FRONT-DOOR SECURITY

Next, consider your arrangements for answering the door. "What?" you say. "Surely, someone knocks on the door and we answer it?" Well, yes, that is what happens when you do not have a Border Terrier. Now that you have taken on the responsibility of a Border, you need to be conscious of where your dog is at all times. I have been told of Borders who have bolted out of an open door in a flash and run away so fast they could not be caught or found. They were then knocked over on the road, or one I was recently told about sadly drowned in a nearby lake.

We never open the front door until we have placed the dogs into a room and shut the door tight, checking that it has closed properly. This might seem like a bit of a time-consuming bind, but it only takes a minute for your Border to slip through that open door and a lifetime of regret to follow. If you have children, it is important that you instil this system into them too, so that when they are running in and out of the house with their friends, they do not let the dog slip out unnoticed. If that is too difficult, then put the dog somewhere safe away from the door while the children are playing.

A danger time, where people have lost their dogs, is when they have been coming in and out of the house, say with shopping from the car. I have spoken to people who are heartbroken to have lost their dogs this way. So

please be extra vigilant at this time and put the dog into another room in the house, away from the opening and closing door.

HIGH-LEVEL DANGER

A small puppy should not be lifted up on to a surface such as a settee and left to explore, as he will surely leap about and try to plummet off the high place as if with a death wish! If children want to play with the puppy, ask them to sit on the floor and let the puppy climb on to their lap. No lifting puppy up, please, as many a small wriggly body has escaped out of a child's arms and fallen to the floor, which can result in severe damage to the puppy – and your purse with vet's fees ensuing.

IN THE GARDEN

So, you think that your house is now secure? Let's move on to the garden. If you are taking a small puppy into your home for the first time, or if it is a while since you had a puppy in the house and garden, you will be amazed at a Border's ability to escape.

Check every inch of the perimeter fence, if you have one, looking for small holes. If you have gates in the garden, are there any small gaps at the bottom? Chicken wire placed at the base of a fence or gate can contain a small puppy, but an older dog can easily rip chicken wire away from the fence if he sees something he considers 'prey', such as a neighbourhood cat or a rodent, or if he sees a bird alight just beyond the fence. We have used weld mesh, which we have stapled to the fence up to a height of about 4 feet (1.3m); the actual fence is about 6 feet high (1.8m), as many a terrier has escaped over fences that were too low.

As this is a determined terrier we are talking about (and some of them can be very determined when it comes to getting 'prey'), we buried the weld mesh under the ground as well. My husband spent all of one summer with his legs sticking out from under the hedges around the garden, while he buried weld mesh into holes he had dug into the ground, back-filling them with concrete or bricks to ensure they stayed in place. If you have a determined digger, then this is necessary, and who is to say, at eight weeks, which puppy will become an escape artist?

What height should your fence be? Well, around 5 to 6 feet (1.5-1.8m) should be satisfactory. I did speak to one lady a while ago who was complaining about her Border bitch escaping out of her garden over a 3-foot (0.9m) fence. As I told her, any self-respecting Border can escape over that height. Remember, they are supposed to be able to go to ground after the fox and jump off and back up on to ledges, using their brains to work their way out

JESSIE: THE ESCAPE ARTIST

I came home from work one day and my father-in-law said one of our Borders, Jessie, had got out of the garden into the field. He did not know how it had happened; he had checked all the fencing and there were no holes in it. I looked out of the window and saw that he been cutting down some branches from the trees and had propped the branches up against the fence as he did so, thereby, I said, making a lovely step-ladder for Jessie, thank you! My father-in-law did not believe that was possible, but oh yes, it was!

of any situations. So, to them, your garden is a puzzle and they are trying to crack it and discover the escape route!

There are dangers of leaving a dog unattended in a garden beyond those of possible escape. A number of Border Terriers have been stolen from gardens, so be on your guard and always know where your dog is at any time.

Border Terriers can be prone to barking at anything passing by, and prolonged barking would not be fair to your neighbours, who have as much right to enjoy their homes and gardens as you have. Our dogs go into the garden to do the necessary and are then brought back into the house.

We would never consider it

wise to use a dog flap so that the dog has access to the garden at all times. This does not train him to be clean in the house (you need to do that by being vigilant and taking him out into the garden yourself when you think he needs to go). A Border will not always come into the warmth and dryness of the house if it rains, snows or is blowing a gale. He may stand in the garden, miserable, wet and cold. I have seen a Border standing outside barking to be let in, when the door to the house was wide open!

One of the worst scenarios that I could imagine with the use of a dog flap is that your Border catches a rat, mouse or bird in the garden and then uses the dog flap to bring the 'prize' into the house. What a lovely welcome home you would have, with bits of flesh, blood and feathers all over the house!

BUYING EQUIPMENT
So, now you want to rush off to the shops and buy your new Border Terrier all the items you need to make him happy!

CRATE
If you plan to invest in a dog crate, there are many places you can purchase one: on the internet, from a specialist

distributor advertising in the dog press, from a local pet shop, and even places such as Argos. Just be sure that the catch is one you can easily open and shut, but that the dog cannot open it from the inside. Border Terriers escape from houses, gardens, and even cages…

I would not recommend the soft cages that have recently come on the market, as a Border could chew his way out of those quite easily, if left unattended. However, some people have used them to good effect for short car journeys (but the crate must be secured safely inside the car so it cannot roll around or become a mobile missile should you be in an accident).

I have recently spoken to someone who owns one of these and she advised that the manufacturers of her soft cage say they are not to be used in cars, so always read the instructions that accompany anything you buy for your Border and adhere to the safety rules.

If you are taking on a puppy, you will need a crate that will be big enough for him when he is fully grown. We use a cage that is larger than he needs, so the water bowl can be clipped at one end and the bedding placed at the other. There is a school of thought that a puppy can be house trained more easily if his bed area is small enough that he does not want to soil it. However, we would rather the puppy take longer to house train and make sure he has enough

If you accustom your Border Terrier to a crate, he will soon look on it as his own special den.

room to stretch out in comfort. In addition, if you need to leave him for a few hours and he has an accident, it is surely better that he can get away from the soiled area and not be uncomfortable all the time you are away from home.

Some people prefer to use a puppy pen – most breeders find them invaluable. But if you have a single puppy, it may be an unnecessary expense and it is probably better to use a crate for the time he is a small puppy.

The cage should never be a

place of punishment, but a place of safety – a den where your Border can go when he is tired. We always put our dogs to bed with a biscuit, and they race to get into their crates, as they want their treats!

CAR TRAVEL

If you can train a baby puppy to use a cage, it will be helpful in the long run, especially when transporting your dog in the car. A loose dog in the car is a danger to himself and the occupants, either by being a distraction to the driver, or by becoming a lethal object in a crash as he hurtles through the air. I once witnessed an accident where two small terriers were thrown through the windscreen of a car and they ran off in pain. They were never found. Whether you decide to use a cage in the car or some sort of dog harness, I would urge you to use something to restrain the dog.

If you use a crate, make sure it is steady and cannot move around in the car. You could place a piece of carpet under the cage, or tie the cage to the inside of the car in some way, or wedge it between other objects – anything so long as it is firmly placed, but not totally covered up. Your dog needs air to breathe, especially on long and/or hot journeys.

I have seen people loading dogs into crates in cars, covering them with coats and other paraphernalia, so much so that the dog could not see out and certainly had no air circulating around him. On a long, hot journey, the dog would certainly be uncomfortable and possibly the journey in those kind of circumstances could be fatal to him. On journeys, make sure your dog is comfortable and that you take frequent stops to let him exercise and relieve himself (cleaning up after him, of course). Take clean, fresh drinking water with you, so he can be cool and watered and enjoy the journey with you.

There are a few essential items to buy before your puppy comes home.

DOG BED

If your preferred bed for your Border Terrier is not a crate, but a dog bed, there are a number of ones you may consider. For a small puppy, I would not recommend one made out of wicker or a beanbag, as they can easily be chewed. With the wicker type, this could be harmful to the puppy, while the bean bag, although comfortable for an older dog who is not a chewer, is easily chewed and the beans spread all over the house. Until you have had a beanbag 'explode', you will not know how difficult it is to collect up those beans, while your puppy is trying to eat them or roller blade on them!

There are some excellent plastic beds, which are easily cleaned should your puppy or dog have an accident. They can be disinfected (but you must make sure you rinse and dry them thoroughly before the puppy is allowed near them again). Inside the bed, you can place one or two comfortable bedding pieces, which can easily be washed in the washing machine after a day or two.

BEDDING

Any dog, but especially a puppy, can soil their bedding, so it is wise to invest in a number of pieces. We use veterinary-type bedding, which is a fleece. But we always check the bedding every morning by feeling and smelling it to see if it is damp or dirty. Vetbed can appear to be clean, as the puppies' urine will

A Border Terrier will enjoy playing with a variety of toys.

go through it, but it is still wet on the top and so, I am afraid, nothing works better than a hand to see if it is dry and a nose to see if it is clean!

We generally have three or more pieces of bedding on the go at one time: one clean piece inside the bed, one just washed and drying, and one new piece waiting to be used.

Border Terriers can and do chew their bedding, so regularly remove any chewed parts. If your puppy has chewed a hole in his bedding, then cut that part away altogether, or throw the bedding away and buy another piece. I have witnessed a dog with her head stuck in a piece of bedding that she had chewed a hole in. It could have been fatal if she had then twisted her body around, so beware of frayed or chewed bedding!

FEEDING BOWLS

There are many types of feeding and water bowls on the market. We like to use a heavy, non-tip bowl for the water; unless you have come back to a room covered in water from a tipped water bowl, you may not appreciate the importance of this. Find a place in the kitchen, or another room where your Border has access to it at all times, in a corner, out of the way of feet (human and canine).

You may consider plastic bowls for food, but if you have a puppy, or an adult who chews, then I would not recommend it. I would invest in metal bowls, which are easily washed.

Remember to wash the bowl immediately after feeding.

GROOMING GEAR

Your Border should be brushed and combed daily. We use a brush for the body and also purchase a comb (to be used after brushing) and also for the head, legs and tail. He will require hand-stripping twice or more a year. You can easily do this yourself with a bit of practice, and perhaps your puppy's breeder may show you how to do this for the first time.

For years we struggled with our dogs on our knees, to strip them, with the dog moving about and hair going everywhere. Then, one year, we invested in a grooming table, which made life a lot easier. You can buy these on-line for a reasonable amount; I believe ours was about £70, but it was definitely worth it, as was the grooming coat I bought a few years ago – no more hairs entwined with jumpers.

For more information on grooming and hand-stripping, see Chapter Five: The Best of Care.

COLLAR AND LEAD

Similarly, there are many types of collar and lead on the market. You will need to change the collar as your puppy grows. You also need to check that the collar, if it is made from nylon or leather, is free from small nicks or stretch marks, as it could snap at a crucial moment.

The lead should also have a secure fastening and be checked regularly. If you decide to buy an extending lead, do not use it by the side of a road, as if it extends there, your Border could run on the road and cause an accident. An extending lead is fine to use in a field or park, but always change to a short lead when going back near a road.

Your dog needs permanent ID in the form of a microchip, and he should also carry contact details on his collar.

your Border does not come to harm.

There are quite a few soft, thin, squeaky toys, which are totally unsuitable for a Border, so although they look fun, remember your dog's safety above all else. The harder and tougher the toy, the better.

For a young puppy, the most safe and enjoyable toys can be found in the house, such as the inside of a toilet roll or paper towel roll, which pup can run about with as his 'toy', and safely chew it up, although you may not find it so much fun to pick up all the pieces!

You should also be sure he does not swallow any matted pieces of soggy paper, as these can get stuck in his mouth and cause him to choke.

ID

In Britain it is a legal requirement for all dogs to be microchipped at eight weeks of age. In addition, dogs must carry a visible from of identification when they are out in public places.

Microchipping involves inserting a microchip, the size of a grain of rice, between the shoulders. This has a unique number which is then matched to your contact details. The chip can be read by a scanner, which means that your dog can always be correctly identified, and you can be reunited if he ever strays or becomes lost.

When your dog is out in public, he should wear a disc, attached to his collar, engraved with your contact details.

TOYS

There is a temptation to buy lots of different toys for your puppy or dog. Some puppies can have one toy for years, while others chew up every toy they are given within a few minutes. It is important that any toy is given under supervision, and that your Border is not left unattended with new toys. If he chews a toy, it could be a hazardous if he swallows all or part of it, causing choking, internal blockages or poisoning. It is amazing what dogs and puppies can chew and swallow, so, if you have children, ensure their toys are put away so

Alternatively, or in addition, you can get your details embroidered on to his collar, which means he still has ID if the disc becomes detached from his collar.

In America dog laws vary between states, so you will need to check what the requirements are in your area.

COLLECTING YOUR PUPPY

At last it is time to collect your puppy. It is best if you arrange to collect him in the morning so he will have all day to play in his new home and adjust to you and your family before bedtime.

The breeder should provide you with Kennel Club registration papers at the time of sale, unless for some reason you have agreed with the breeder that this particular puppy is being bought without registration papers. There is nothing wrong with a breeder withholding papers, as long as you have both agreed that this would take place. It is better to have this in writing and some breeders will prepare an agreement between the breeder and puppy purchaser.

The other paperwork you may expect to receive from the breeder, includes a three-, four- or five-generation pedigree for

FINDING A VET

If you live near your breeder, ask them which vet they use and consider going there. Otherwise, there are various methods of finding a vet. You could look in the Yellow Pages, or, better still, ask friends and relatives who live nearby and have pets for a recommendation.

Register your puppy with the vet as soon as you collect him. It is always preferable to have the vet look at your puppy promptly (say, the next day), rather than waiting until you have fallen in love with him, only to find he has some health problems. If at any time you are not happy with something your vet is doing or saying, firstly ask for further clarification (it may be that you have just not understood the reasons behind what is happening) and then do not be afraid to ask for a second opinion. Your vet should not mind.

the puppy, a receipt for the money you have paid, details of when and with what he was wormed (should be at least three times, if he is an eight- week-old puppy), and a diet sheet that shows what he is fed on and how many times a day. An eight-week-old puppy will be on three or four meals a day.

The breeder should also give you a small supply of food for the puppy, so that you may continue to use the same diet. Too many changes are not good for the puppy; he should have as many constants at this time as

possible, including food!

If you must change his food, then discuss this with his breeder and only do so gradually over a week or two, adding one-third new food to two-thirds old for a few days, then half and half, and then two-thirds new and one-third old, and then on to the new food regime. Do not chop and change his food all the time, as you could upset his stomach and make him faddy about his food. For information on feeding, see Chapter Five.

MEETING THE FAMILY

When you take the puppy or older dog home, it is a major change to his lifestyle.

He is coming into a strange house, with new rules and different people; he has lost his siblings and his dam and may be a little over-awed. Try not to have all and sundry come to visit in those first few days. It is a temptation to show off your new acquisition, but too many comings and goings will make it harder for the pup to settle into his new routine.

Ask people to stay away for a few weeks, until he has settled in, especially if they have dogs of their own at home, as they could bring in viruses to your unvaccinated puppy. They should stay away, in that case, until he has had all his injections and you should not take him out of the house and garden until your vet advises you that it is safe to do so.

CHILDREN

If you have small children, you should already have taught them how to behave around the puppy before you bring him home. There should be no shrieking and shouting, no pulling and tugging on him, and no picking him up. A good start would be to teach your children to respect the dog and care for him. If they want to hold him, they should be asked to sit on the floor and let him climb on their laps, but only if he wants to.

A puppy should not be forced to stay with children, as, if he is scared, he only has two options: fight or flight! If he seems unsure, wait until he is feeling more confident, and explain to the children how important it is to make the puppy feel comfortable in his new home.

I do get a lot of anxious people, worried about their Border puppy biting them and the children, and tugging on their trousers and socks etc. This is a phase they go through and while you need to stop it and teach the children how to get out of the way and not make it worse by shrieking and playing tug-of-war with the puppy, you do not need to make a huge problem out of it (see Mouthing, page 66). The needle-sharp puppy teeth will drop out at around four or five months and this desire to sink their teeth into everything will diminish.

Small children should never be left alone with a dog. You should supervise their interactions at all times.

At last, the big day arrives and it is time to collect your puppy.

OTHER DOGS

If you are bringing a puppy into a home where there is an adult dog, be aware that the older pet may be used to having your sole attention; it is going to take some time, perhaps weeks, for him to get used to having another animal in the house. Do not worry if he seems less than impressed at the outset and seems to wonder when this young upstart is going home.

Make sure the puppy cannot steal the adult dog's food and be aware that the adult dog should, at least at this stage, be the dominant one over the puppy. Puppy teeth are very sharp and you can expect the adult dog to chastise the puppy if he oversteps the mark in rough play. Try not to interfere too much, and do not tell the adult dog off for putting the puppy in his place. Allow the older dog to display natural dominance over the younger one, unless you feel the puppy really is in danger.

It is important that the adult dog has some time alone with you (such as when the pup is in his crate) a few times a day, especially if your existing dog is elderly. Do not let the puppy spend all day chasing the adult dog around, as even the most placid of dogs may get a little fed up with this.

If you have other dogs and you are bringing an adult dog into the home, it is important that they meet on neutral territory, with as much quiet as possible. Do not make a large

Children and Border Terriers are a great mix – as long as mutual respect is established.

fuss about the meeting and, of course, if you know that your existing dog is nervous or aggressive around other dogs, it is not a good idea to get another one. After initial introductions, monitor the

situation closely, but without getting uptight about it; keep a calm attitude and, hopefully, all will be well. Separate the newcomer at bedtime, at least initially, until he has become an accepted member of the pack.

OTHER PETS

Border Terriers and cats can exist peaceably together, but you need to gauge the situation. If you have a cat in the house when you acquire your puppy, then usually the cat will be the boss and will put the puppy in his place. Once he learns that the cat has claws and will swipe at him, he may defer to it and grow up living side by side in harmony. Although he may still view the next-door cat as prey...

If you are bringing an adult Border into a house with a cat, you will need to be more careful. If the Border does not like cats, or has been used to chasing them out of his garden in his previous home, he could easily kill a cat. Always ensure the cat has a way of getting out of the room – for example, by using baby gates to keep the dog in the room while allowing the cat to leave it. Feed the cat in a different place, where the dog has no access, so that he does not steal the cat's food.

If you have other smaller critters in the house, such as hamsters and gerbils, you will need to be much more careful. If you have children, they will not like to witness their Border killing their other pets, but that is more than a possibility and the dog should not be blamed for doing what comes naturally. So, the answer is to be vigilant at all times.

I sold a Border bitch to a friend and, in due course, the bitch had a litter of puppies. There was an adult female cat in the house and she gave birth to a litter of kittens around the same time, but sadly mother cat died in a car accident shortly after the kittens were born. My friend put the kittens in with the Border bitch and she accepted them, fed and raised them. The kittens were rehomed when they were weaned, apart from Ben, a big, black cat, who would swagger into the kitchen, thinking he was in charge of all the dogs. Because he was a very confident cat, he never had a problem with any dog chasing him, and they would all rush up and submit to him!

THE FIRST NIGHT

If you have brought your puppy home in the early part of the day, that will give him plenty of time to adjust to his new home before bedtime. Give him some food, take him out to the garden for toileting, and pop him in his crate with a safe toy that he cannot destroy or choke on, and leave him there. If there are children in the house, tell them to leave him quietly alone. If you can do that a couple of times during the first day, then by bedtime he will be a little more reassured than if he were put into it in the dark, on his own, for the first time.

A Border will make friends with the family cat – but he will still see the neighbours' cats as fair prey.

Some people put a hot-water bottle in with the puppy (but it must be securely wrapped up so as not to burn him) and leave a radio playing low, or a clock ticking somewhere close to where he is sleeping. Others take the crate into their bedroom for the first few nights or weeks, until the puppy has settled into his new home.

HOUSE TRAINING

A small puppy needs taking out at regular hourly intervals. In addition, he should always be taken out after eating, after playing, and when he wakes from a sleep. Take him to the same area in the garden, and stay with him until he performs. Then give him lots of praise, and maybe have a game with him before returning to the house. When your puppy is getting the idea, you can introduce a command, such as "Busy", to encourage the pup to perform. Never scold your puppy for making mistakes in the house; they are all your fault for not anticipating his actions and reactions.

Never leave your puppy for extended periods in a small crate. At eight weeks, they need to 'go' frequently, so please do not blame the puppy if you go to him in the morning and he has made a mess in his bed or cage. Obviously, a small puppy cannot be expected to be clean overnight to begin with, but as he grows up a little he will soon get the idea of not soiling his bed.

If you have given a home to an adult dog, he may be upset at the change in environment and this could result in a break down of his house-training. All you need to do is to go back to basics: quietly show him where to perform and praise him when he gets it right. If you treat him kindly, and he understands what is required, he will soon get back on track.

FIRST LESSONS

It is important to establish house rules so that your Border understands what is, and what is not, allowed. If there are areas of the house that you want to keep dog-free, then all the family need to be consistent in this. Train the family to train the dog; you cannot expect your dog to stick to the rules if everyone is giving him different instructions!

When you have a new puppy or rehome an adult dog, you should try to find out a little about his previous home. If you are buying a puppy, was he reared in the house or outside? Is he used to being handled? Love and consistency, with a small dose of rules thrown in, is the order of the day. Never allow any member of the family to tease your Border, playing rough games of tug-of-war, or allowing him to chase and nip. What may be appealing with an eight-week-old puppy may not be so appealing in an adult dog. In

To begin with, a puppy will miss the companionship of his littermates.

Take your puppy to an allocated toileting area in the garden, and he will soon learn what is required.

particular, ensure children do not tease the dog, as he may grow to resent them. Children and Border Terriers can be a lovely combination, but only if the children respect the puppy.

HANDLING

Your Border needs to accept all-over handling so that he can be groomed or examined by a vet when necessary. Right from the start, slowly and gently get the puppy used to being brushed and combed. Remember, you are the one in charge of everything that happens to your dog, not him. You should never say: "He will not let me brush him", or "He does not like being taken off

the bed". You decide where he goes and what he does. As long as you are not hurting him, then you need to start as you mean to go on and brush and comb him every day, right from day one. The Border Terrier has a strong character and it is important to establish your leadership right from the start.

You will also need to check his ears, eyes and paws on a daily basis. It is a good plan to trim nails once a week so that your puppy gets used to the attention. If he is a very young puppy, just take the edge of the nails off with human nail clippers, so he gets used to having it done, and reward him with a treat. Do not

make a big fuss, just do the job quickly and calmly, and your Border will realise there is nothing to worry about. Someone once told me they could not brush an eight-week-old puppy, as he would not let them do it – and six months later, he was a handful of spit and fire to get his nails clipped. "He will not let..." should not be in your vocabulary.

MOUTHING

A small puppy may try to mouth you, as he would his littermates. There is no need to punish this with harshness, but you should just say "Ouch" or "No" in a firm way, and then distract the puppy

HANDLING AND GROOMING

Accustom your Border Terrier to being handled and groomed at an early stage.

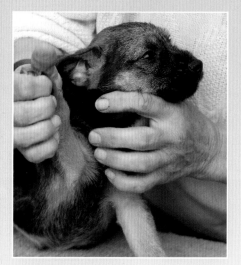

Lift up each paw in turn.

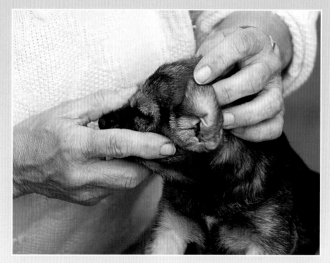

Check the inside of the ears.

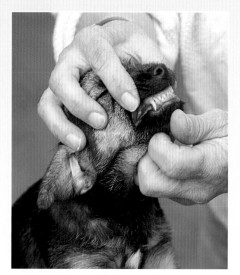

Part the mouth so you can examine teeth and gums.

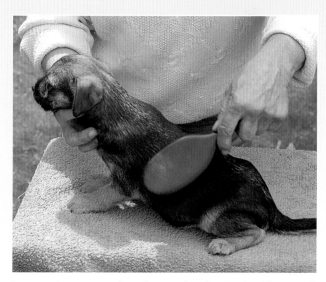

A puppy does not need much grooming, but he should get used to the feel of a brush and comb.

Provide toys and chews for your puppy while he is teething.

with a toy. We never wear shoes with laces when we have litters of puppies, and do not have loose flapping trousers, which are very enticing to a baby puppy. Do not worry too much about mouthing at this stage. I have talked to many people who were really worried that they had a 12-week-old monster on their hands, but by the time the puppy had finished teething, by four or five months, he had stopped this behaviour.

Puppy teeth are very sharp, and children may shriek and run if the puppy is after their trainers or pulling at their clothes, but such behaviour only exacerbates the situation. You need to supervise all interactions, making sure children do not get over-excited, and putting a stop to the puppy chasing or mouthing.

I spoke to a lady recently who could not control her puppy and stop it biting her trouser legs, so she was walking across the floor, dragging the puppy with her, attached to her trousers, as he play-growled and bit her. This is not the correct way to deal with a puppy. Dragging him along only makes the 'game' more fun for him. You need to stand still, remove him, say "no" and distract him with a toy or ball. If you do not have one to hand, carry him to where they are and then throw them for him.

Do not take part in tugging games with tug ropes. These become games of dominance, which he would do with his siblings; he should not be allowed to do this with you,

unless you 'win' every time. They can also damage his teeth and, if he swallows part of the rope, they can wrap around his intestines and he will require an operation. There is an excellent discussion on this normal puppy problem in a section headed "Biting" on Border Terrier World (http://www.borderterrierworld. co.uk/), a discussion forum for Border owners.

WEARING A COLLAR
Well before the time your puppy is ready to be taken out for a walk, you should introduce him to a collar. I buy a small, soft collar and put it on the puppy for an hour or so at a time, preferably when he is distracted with something else, so that he forgets about it. Make sure the

Life will never be the same once a Border Terrier has become part of your family.

collar is not too tight, and never leave it on when a puppy is unsupervised, as it could get caught up in something.

The baby collar can be used, at hourly intervals, for a month or two, and the puppy will then be perfectly happy to wear a collar in the future. But always consider removing the collar when he is in the house, especially if there are other dogs present, or he is unsupervised, as a number of dogs have caught their collars on items in the house or on another dog's teeth, some with fatal results.

Remember to change the size of collar as the puppy grows: a very important and simple point, but sometimes forgotten. For more information on training, see Chapter Six.

GETTING USED TO THE CAR
Make the first car journeys short, broken up with a walk in the park or field, so that the puppy associates the car with a pleasant experience. Take some paper towels and old towels with you, in case the puppy is sick, as many are on their first journey.

We carry a few things in our car, which come in handy. They include: a bowl for water; a large bottle of water for drinks, and for cleaning the dog should he roll in fox dirt or anything else that Border Terriers love to roll in.

You will also need some paper towels, and an old towel or two for drying him off; a plastic bag to place the offensive material once you have cleaned him

(until you have smelt fox dirt in the car on the way home, you will not know why!); and baby wipes, to try to remove some of that smell before you can get him home for a wash down. We also have a spray bottle with diluted tee tree oil (it must be diluted, or else it could damage his skin) for the extra-offensive smells.

Finally, enjoy your travels through life with your Border. It will be an interesting and worthwhile journey, with lots of fun along the way. Your Border Terrier should not dictate the speed at which you travel, or the direction in which you head, but be sure that he will stay with you to the end, a loyal and loving companion for all his life. Good luck!

THE BEST OF CARE

Chapter 5

The Border Terrier is a hardy breed, and, with commonsense, he is easy to look after. However, like all animals, he has specific needs and it is important that owners are able to give the best possible care.

FEEDING ISSUES

Most dogs are greedy by nature. Picking up food whenever it is available is a primal urge because a dog never knows when the next meal may come along. Most Border Terriers will fill their boots at the drop of a hat. Scientific dietary requirements never list such delights as cat poo, sheep poo, chewing gum and sometimes each other's poo. A Border Terrier has very catholic tastes and, amazingly, they never seem the worse for the experience.

Many pet dog owners will tell

you that their fat dog is always hungry and they must keep feeding him because he wants food. This is especially true of Border Terrier owners, who constantly give in to the winning ways of their pet – the appealing expression, the begging, the staring – willing you to part with food.

We live in a time when we humans tend to over-eat and the pet Border is a classic example of the side-kick, showing signs of little exercise with a girth that goes with too much grub. Show exhibitors try to keep their charges in perfect body for show purposes, and diet is adjusted according to performance and appearance. But some pet owners buy a companion, and soon the Border Terrier starts to be treated as a small person living in the house, who is often fed without regard to his essential needs.

SO WHERE DO WE BEGIN?

Many years ago, dogs were fed on human food scraps; most did well, but some were cruelly neglected. It is perfectly possible to feed dogs an unbalanced diet and keep them alive. However, it is our responsibility to ensure that, if we are to keep a dog, his basic needs are catered for. That means food, shelter, warmth and human company. Border Terriers are sociable dogs and they like to be indoors, which immediately answers three of the basic requirements. However, his food is often something that is added to the supermarket list rather than part of a special research trip to the pet shop.

BASIC GUIDELINES

You may feel baffled by the choice of dog food available, but there are some basic guidelines that are worth following:

A Border Terrier will try to convince you that he is always hungry...

- Like their owners, no two Border Terriers are the same, and one food type may not suit every dog. A caring owner will recognise this and act accordingly.
- Cheap foods are not necessarily the best. Clearly, if the advertised food is very cheap, then its ingredients are most likely to be of poorer quality.
- Many dry foods contain coloured dyes – which are not much good to dogs, who are colour blind. To obtain nourishment from cheap food, it's necessary to feed more of it, which usually produces more unpleasant stools to pick up and a dog in poor condition.
- What goes in one end comes out at the other. Looking at the excrement produced by your Border is an instant indication of his well-being. He shouldn't be pooing every time he goes out: two or three times a day is normal. Stools should be firm, and he shouldn't have to strain to produce one. Soft stools, which are difficult to pick up and bin, or have a mucus content, are not the stools of a healthy dog. Make sure you check your dog's stools regularly, and if they are not firm, ask yourself if it could be because of his diet.

MARKET FORCES

What should we feed? With so many pet foods on the market, the choice is bewildering. Every manufacturer advertises something special about the food it produces, and all have the potential to fatten or fill.

The big manufacturers rely on exposure of their brand through advertising and marketing, to ensure that dog owners recall and recognise the brand when they go shopping. For example, most keen dog owners who watch Crufts on television will be very aware of the Pedigree brand sponsorship. Its regular advertising on TV, voucher inserts in magazines and the company's high profile on the supermarket shelves ensures that everyone with an interest in dogs knows the brand and, when prompted, will mention it.

Competition between the big dog food producers is huge, and millions of pounds are spent in pursuit of your cash. Focus groups discuss products with dog owners, surveys are carried out in supermarkets, and on-the-spot surveys are conducted in the street. With the larger companies, nothing is left to chance. You may receive a newsletter through the post, free samples, or a coupon in a magazine in a bid to make you buy a particular product.

There are many choices out there, including tinned meats, dried meats, kibbles, biscuits and mixers, complete foods, moist foods and wet foods. The choice is infinite and you, the owner, are confronted by rows and rows of excellent packaging, designed to catch your eye, with "so much off", "33 per cent extra free", "buy one, get one free" and "buy this and get a free chew". If Border Terriers didn't have such cast-iron constitutions, here are many opportunities for digestive disorders.

Carbohydrates are needed for energy – the amount required depends on a dog's lifestyle.

A WELL-BALANCED DIET

This depends primarily on the dog breed and its size. Border Terriers are classed as a medium/small breed, and their needs are relatively easy to cater for. Too many calories will make a Border very obese. Like the dog itself, balance is the key. There are a number of components needed in a well-balanced diet:

PROTEIN

Every dog needs protein to provide the amino acids that they themselves cannot make in their bodies. A good-quality dog food will have all the necessary proteins to enable the dog's body to make the conversion from food into energy.

A dog will always choose a high-protein snack if he finds one outdoors. Dead animals, stomach contents and even vegetables are attractive.

Puppies, pregnant and lactating bitches, and growing dogs all need more protein in their diet. Conversely, foods can be fed with a lower protein content if the dog is a total couch potato.

CARBOHYDRATES

Carbohydrates are nutrients derived from plants and include starches, sugars, cereals and plant fibre. Corn, wheat and soya contain protein and are often used in dog foods. Carbohydrates also serve as a back-up source of energy.

Dog that are extremely active (e.g. Foxhounds, sled dogs, working collies, field trialling dogs and even Border Terriers taking part in agility) may need more than just a balanced diet, as they have increased energy requirements. They may need more carbohydraters after such intense bouts of exercise. A normally active Border will need about 36 per cent of carb content in his daily diet.

Glycogen, which is made from glucose molecules stored in the muscles and the liver, is a principal fuel for dogs. However, their bodies can only store small amounts so the store is soon depleted. A normal, balanced diet can replace the used glycogen in about 24 hours, but for madly active dogs, additional carbohydrate help may be needed. This can be given as honey mixed with water or by other means, such as wholegrain cereals, although the latter can take much longer to be digested and converted.

Dietary fibre is plant material made up of carbohydrates and is good for intestinal health. Fruits or vegetables can be added to any food as a good source of fibre. A number of dried kibble foods now contain potato or rice in some form, either rice with chicken or lamb, or rice with fish. Instead of feeding dog biscuits, which are always fattening and

not always good for canine teeth, feed raw or par-boiled vegetables or fruit – a good treat with no added calories.

Sudden changes in carbohydrate type or quantity can cause loose stools or diarrhoea. As a generalisation, dry dog foods contain between 30 per cent and 60 per cent carbohydrates, and canned foods have up to 30 per cent.

ESSENTIAL FATS

Essential fats from animal fat and plant seed oils are used as an energy source. Fatty acids carry fat-soluble vitamins around the body while, at the same time,

building growth. Fatty acids are vital for skin health, which is why puppies should always be fed with suitably formulated puppy foods to prevent dry skins and poor coats. It is not only humans who need omega-3 in their diets; dogs also need it to help their eyesight and their brain power.

VITAMINS/MINERALS

Vitamins are very important in a dog's diet, as a deficiency can give rise to a number of ailments, with far-reaching consequences. For example, vitamin A loss can lead to vision impairment, skin lesions, infections and respiratory ailments.

HOW MUCH TO FEED

The average daily energy need of any 4.5 kg (10lb) dog varies according to its lifestyle:

- An inactive dog (i.e not very active at all) only needs 296 calories each day
- An adult active dog (i.e. companion dogs who takes country walks etc) needs 404 calories each day
- A pregnant bitch (from 4 weeks after mating to whelping) needs 518 calories each day
- A young active dog needs 436 calories per day
- And an older active dog needs 327 calories per day

Because of decreased physical activity and slowed metabolism, older active dogs need 20

per cent fewer total calories than do young or middle-aged adult dogs. As dogs age, they tend to become overweight. It may take obese dogs longer for their blood glucose concentrations to return to normal. This disrupted carbohydrate metabolism can lead to diabetes.

*1 calorie =1 kilocalorie = 1,000 calories. The term 'calorie' that is used on food nutrition labels is really a 'food calorie' – sometimes called a 'large calorie'. It is equivalent to 1,000 calories (or 1 kilocalorie), as calories are defined scientifically (the amount of energy needed to warm 1 gram of water 1°C).

(Data from the National Academy of Sciences 2006 - the Nutrient Requirements of Dogs and Cats)

COMPLETE DIETS

A complete food is exactly what it says it is – complete. At huge development expense, manufacturers have come up with a food that answers all the essential requirements of the modern dog. Not only is it complete, but there are now variations of food type and shape to suit various breeds of dog, designed to help different face and jaw constructions, and to make it easier for that particular dog to pick up and eat his food. No such expense needs to be expended on a Border. Point him at a dish and he will find a way to eat it – faster than anyone can utter the words, "Can he manage his meal in that dish?"

As discussed earlier, the cheaper the food, the more likely it is that it will be less nutritious for the dog. Coloured biscuit is just coloured biscuit in any bag. Look at the Typical Analysis per 100g label on the side or the back of the food bag, not the colourful picture and copy on the front. It will tell you how much fat, protein and mineral is present in the complete food. If your dog needs to lose weight, remember that the feeding guides are based on a dog's target weight, not its actual weight.

My own dogs are given one particular complete brand, which, over recent years, I have found is consistent and on which they thrive and do well. The ingredients comprise: a minimum of 63 per cent brown rice, a minimum of 20 per cent chicken (it is described as a chicken and brown rice complete food), oats, peas, chicken oil, sunflower oil, seaweed, minerals and vitamins and nothing else.

The packaging also offers the following advice for those changing diets to this complete food: "Unless otherwise recommended, introduce your dog to a new diet gradually over 7-10 days. Mix a little of the new food with the former diet, gradually altering the proportions until only the new food is being fed. This (sic) is a complete, balanced high-quality food for all adult dogs, including seniors, and it is intended to satisfy requirements for maintenance. The food contains all essential nutrients and therefore the use of vitamin and mineral supplements is not recommended."

When they have been very well behaved (which, you will appreciate, is rarely), I give my Borders a complete snack food, which is a hard-baked brown rice and fish biscuit – and they love them. They are also perfect for keeping teeth clean.

Feeding complete food doesn't mean that your Border can't enjoy par-boiled vegetables, such as broccoli, cabbage, swede and other vegetables and fruits. Of course he can – perhaps as a snack food.

Feeding a Border is easy, as he will eat everything. The trick is to ensure he gets just enough and that what he gets is good, nourishing food to nurture the body and keep him fit.

A complete food may not be the convenient answer for everyone. Some owners like to be more creative, and there are plenty of alternative food types from which to choose.

A complete diet is manufactured to meet all your dog's nutritional needs.

Tinned food is fed with a mixer biscuit.

Lack of vitamin E can lead to muscle breakdown, reproductive failure and retinal degeneration. Thiamin (an additive in many of our morning cereals) loss can cause brain damage if the deprivation is sudden, and can cause death or heart damage if the loss is chronic. Vitamin D, on the other hand, can be toxic if used excessively.

CHOOSING A DIET

A diet must be correctly balanced, but choice is also dictated by the owner's lifestyle. A busy owner finds it easier to open a pouch of moist food or use a complete food rather than cook meat or prepare a special diet for the family pet.
There are pros and cons involved in feeding the different types of diet:

HOMEMADE

In the 1970s, my dogs were fed exclusively on a cereal meal (there were few complete foods available then), with cracked or soft eggs from the local farm twice a week, and vegetable leftovers from the garden. My Border Terriers have always been great foragers, enjoying strawberries, raspberries, gooseberries, blackcurrants, redcurrants, apples, broccoli and other green vegetables at will – in fact, whatever is in season.

When, some years later, they were working, doing the job they were bred to do – bolting foxes – we were often given off-cuts from fallen stock given to the hunt kennels nearby. Occasionally, we would be given a skinned calf or a sheep. Once the meat was taken off the bones, the bones were scraped down and given to the dogs to enjoy for a couple of days. Then they were collected up and boiled to remove the marrow and other nutrients. The resulting cooled jelly was used to mix with the cereal meal and the eggs, and this would be fed until the jelly was finished.

All the meat was cut up into small portions, bagged and frozen until required. The bags would be thawed out and the meat cooked as required – again mixed with the cereal, par-boiled greens, turnips, swedes, and anything else the dogs could crunch and enjoy.

When fed this diet the dogs' teeth were always white and clean, and their stools were firm and infrequent. There were no anal gland problems and their coats were in great condition.

I am not nostalgic for those days of boning out carcases and labouring over boilers. Why should any of us have to do that when kind manufacturers do it for us and produce food in sanitised bags, all ready to dish up as needed?

CANNED FOOD

Commercial canned dog food can contain up to 75 per cent moisture, and most canned food has relatively more fat and protein and fewer carbohydrates than does dry and semi-moist food, and it generally contains much higher levels of animal products.

Pet food labels must list the percentage of protein, fat, fibre and water in the food. When reading labels, it is important to remember that what may appear to be a big difference in the amount of a nutrient — for example, 8 per cent protein in a canned dog food versus 27 per cent protein in a dry dog food — actually reflects the fact that canned food contains a great deal of moisture.

In these days of waste disposal concerns, the washing out of cans and their careful disposal, plus the greater convenience of dried foods, canned dog foods may soon disappear. However, it is always a question of personal choice. A thieving Border is less likely to break into a can – although I do know some who have – and cans may be handy or convenient when dealing with just one dog.

I do keep tinned dog food and a small bag of regular broken biscuit meal in the kennels for the odd time when my regular dog food delivery may fail for any reason. The dogs regard occasions when tinned tripe is given as a bonus. I used to feed green (untreated) tripe when I could get it, but it is such an odious food to serve up unless absolutely fresh that I abandoned this avenue fairly early in my dog breeding career.

RAW FOOD

It is becoming an increasingly popular option to feed raw food. This system of feeding – publicised as the BARF diet (Biologically Appropriate Raw Food) – mimics the diet of wild dogs, using available raw foodstuffs. Ingredients include muscle, meat, bone, fat, offal and vegetable materials.

Initially, owners had to source the raw food, but now it is widely available in a manufactured, minced form which you can keep in the freezer. This makes it more convenient to feed, and it is more manageable for small

There is increasing interest in providing a more natural diet.

Nutritional needs change as a puppy grows and matures.

breeds. Many owners add raw vegetables, such as carrot, cabbage or broccoli, to the diet.

Fans of raw feeding claim it results in healthier, cleaner teeth, improves digestion, produces firmer stools and also reduces allergies.

CALORIE VALUES

Manufacturers of treats and titbits are not legally bound to state the nutritional benefits of their product – so overfeed at your peril.

Common sense is so important. After slowly introducing a new food until your dog is solely fed on the new product, follow the manufacturer's advised portions and watch your dog's appearance. We discussed earlier in this chapter the importance of checking his stools – that they are formed and firm. But what about his general appearance? Does he look too thin – can you see his ribs? Is he becoming too fat and lethargic?

I consider that a normally healthy dog needs at least one month on a new food for the benefits to begin to show. A Border's topcoat should be coarse and harsh – but not completely dead and stiff. He should be fit and active; eyes bright and always ready to exercise.

If you feel that the results are not as you would wish, either reduce or step up the quantities directed on the pack. Remember that the quantities are a guide only, and, like people, the metabolism in dogs varies from individual to individual.

CHANGING NEEDS

Older dogs need fewer calories, for the simple reason that they are less active – they don't burn up as many calories. By contrast, young puppies need plenty of calories to help them grow and to support them while they exercise and play.

When puppies are born and start to take their mother's milk, they benefit from the dam's colostrum (first milk), giving them essential antibodies, protecting them from infection and kick-starting their digestive systems.

Once they are weaned, ideally at four weeks – depending on the size of the litter and the demands on the dam – they can start on formulated puppy food but should still have access to their mother's milk. Worming, using a propriety product, should start at two weeks and continue until the puppies leave home. For my own dogs, I start at two weeks, then four, eight, 12 and 24 weeks. Thereafter, at six-monthly intervals throughout their lives.

I feed the dam cooked pasta, cooked white rice with white meat or fish over the first few days after whelping until she is more relaxed and back to a settled routine again. Basically, I give anything appropriate that is gentle on her digestion, including the formulated puppy diet.

Years ago, puppies didn't always survive to maturity and many were born weak. Litters rarely produce runts these days,

When a puppy first arrives in his new home, he will need four meals a day.

because the modern Border generally gets the best of everything and mortality rates are extremely low. Consequently, these larger litters can be demanding on the mother, so she should be encouraged to eat little and often, with plenty of nourishing proteins and iron-making foods. Fruit and vegetables are also good for her at this time. My nursing bitches have whatever they want, based around a complete food for regular meals and as many treats in between as they want.

FEEDING PUPPIES

I know many people who feel more comfortable feeding Weetabix, ground mince, eggs, fish and combinations of these when rearing a litter of Borders. This food preparation is time-consuming, and new owners may

find it easier to give a simpler food that complements their busy lifestyles. With the huge choice of formulated puppy feeds from the big manufacturers on the market to suit all breeds of puppies, there is no necessity to feed a homemade diet, unless it's a question of personal preference. Bear in mind that a growing Border puppy needs roughly twice as many calories per pound of bodyweight as an adult.

As an owner, you will "get out what you put in", and there is no better start for a puppy than complete mother's milk and then the best formulated complete puppy food you can buy. My puppies go straight from mother's milk to pre-soaked complete puppy food, which contains the correct balance of minerals, proteins and vitamins. I have used it for many puppies

DENTAL HEALTH

One important feature to note when feeding your Border Terrier is that prepared dog foods, such as canned and complete diets, do not naturally clean a dog's teeth. Some of the largest veterinary expenses for the family pet in mid to later life is dentistry work.

Years ago, dogs could be given a large bone from the butcher – but nowadays getting hold of bones is almost impossible. So, once again, the dog food manufacturers have filled the gap by creating dental chewsticks that clean the teeth. There is a further choice – buying canine toothpaste with a thimble-style applicator from your vet, and gently brushing the teeth as soon as the adult set appear.

Don't neglect your Border's teeth, as discolouration can cause a build-up of tartar and plaque, ultimately leading to dental troubles. But remember never to feed cooked bones of any sort: they can splinter inside the mouth, tear the throat tissue or get stuck in the gut.

JUNIOR TO ADULT

As five/six months approaches, teeth will start to drop out and the adult set of teeth appear. My puppies will be wormed again at this point, after which I will begin introducing a different adult food. It now becomes a personal preference for you as the owner. There are puppy diets that cater for juniors up to 18 months, but I prefer to move a youngster over gradually to adult food before he reaches 12 months. This is because Border Terriers mature quite early and usually 'finish' (i.e. mature) at about two years of age.

FEEDING REGIMES

There is a school of thought that supports free feeding, which is when food is constantly available. I am not in favour of this method. Leaving food down encourages laziness and it also poses a health hazard. Dishes left around containing food encourage vermin, and food loses its freshness. If food is not eaten, it makes it difficult to establish if a Border is sick and off his food, or just being over-fed.

I feed my adults once a day, but if I think that one of the terriers is looking a bit on the thin side, I also feed a small morning meal until I am satisfied that his condition has improved. A normal, healthy adult dog will clean up every time, and the dishes can be washed immediately after feeding and put away again.

If ever a Border Terrier leaves

and have never had a bad reaction – and they love it. By the time they are ready to leave for their new homes, they will be eating four meals a day and will rarely go to the dam for top-ups.

Owners should be given diet and general guidance notes, plus samples of the food. This should include the correct amount of prepared or pre-soaked food as a guide to how much the puppy needs at each mealtime, and the other may be a dry version of the same food. By 12 weeks the puppies should be enjoying dry meals – with plenty of available drinking water. I encourage owners to call me to discuss any

diet queries, including the addition of other foods, and/or the change from the puppy food to an adult alternative. By the time the Border is 10-12 months he will have graduated to an adult dietary regime with two small meals or one larger meal per day.

With a new puppy, it is very important to establish a routine, and diet is a crucial part of that regime. The change of home and the loss of his siblings, plus strange new owners is traumatic enough, so it is vital that the diet remains exactly the same for at least a few weeks while he settles in.

his food, I know there is something wrong and I go into 'monitoring mode'. If a tempting morsel or two doesn't switch him on again, it's a stools and urine check, full body inspection and, if I am still uncertain, a veterinary appointment. I will watch a dog for a couple of days before I take him to the vet, to try to establish the reason for the lack of appetite. Watch for obvious signs of pain, discharge, tenderness anywhere, possible blockages, etc. It's always better to be able to give your vet some clues if your Border is off-colour – and being off his food is a sure sign of being unwell.

DIET SWITCHING

So, there is a special offer on at the supermarket and you can save some cash on a different dog food from your tried-and-trusted make. It is an introductory offer and your Border Terrier might like it, so you buy a bag.

OK, but remember that you never get enough in a trial bag to be able to make an informed decision about the benefits or otherwise of the new food. A dog needs at least a month on a new food to establish its worth, in my opinion. It takes time for the ingredients to be assimilated into the system and for the results to be seen in the coat, breath, urine, stools and general well-being.

It is never a good idea to remove an acceptable food source from a dog immediately, however good the alternative

If you feed your dog treats, they should be deducted from his daily ration.

A Border Terrier should be kept in lean, muscular condition.

FAT DOGS

We are getting fatter as a human race in the Western world, and our dogs are getting fatter, too. We have too much choice and eat too much rubbish. We snack and graze during the day, and give our Border Terriers plenty of our foods as they keep us company. What you see in your dog is the direct result of calories in and calories out. Too many calories into a dog who has little exercise equals an obese dog.

Combine that with the endless choice of pet foods available, and the task of keeping dogs fit and healthy can be daunting for the pet owner.

How do you know if your Border Terrier is overweight? If you can't feel his ribs; if you can't see his waist when you look down on him from above; if you can see fatty rolls under his skin – he's fat.

If your Border resembles this description, then it's time you took him in hand or you will shorten his life and have a sick dog for most of his old age. Your vet can help by weighing him and advising on a strict diet, suggesting suitable food and advocating regular weigh-ins at the surgery.

Complete foods always have a feeding guide that often suggests more than is required. An obese dog needs less food and, if possible, should be switched to a low calorie complete food. No table scraps and no 'guilt-prompted' alternatives.

Obesity is particularly damaging in older dogs, who

appears to be. It should always be a gradual switch. Add a little of the new food to each meal until the new food is the main ingredient in the dish. Before buying, check the protein levels to ensure they are compatible with those of the current food.

TREATS

Treats are a thorny issue. Owners give cups of tea, toast, biscuits and any manner of human foods to their charges, all of which are fine – in moderation.

Absolute no-nos for all dogs are raisins, currants, grapes and chocolate – especially dark chocolate, which is poisonous and can put a dog into a coma very quickly.

My own dogs have one dog biscuit each when they are left, and when they go to bed at night – and no more. I buy smoked bones (at a ridiculous price) and they enjoy chewing them during the day. If I am cooking, they get raw or par-boiled vegetable scraps. Hide chews are also popular, but buy a reputable brand – some imported chews are not good quality, and small chews can cause a dog to choke.

need 20 per cent fewer calories than adult Border Terriers, but they also need more protein. It takes a fat dog much longer to assimilate food, and for the blood glucose concentrations to return to normal. As a consequence, an overweight dog is more likely to develop diabetes.

GROOMING YOUR BORDER TERRIER

Caring for a Border Terrier is all about observation. I always watch my dogs very carefully, monitoring what they eat, the condition of their stools, and how they look. When I groom a Border, I can assess the coats and the skin. A Border's coat should never be shiny. It should have a thick undercoat like that of a rabbit, which keeps him warm, and a coarse topcoat (like coconut matting), which is waterproof and is expendable when the Border is doing his job underground, rubbing against stones and tree roots.

Because there is very little underground action for Border Terriers these days, we have to manually strip off the old coat twice a year. This is a finger-and-thumb job, which may take some time.

DAILY GROOMING

Brushing your Border once a day will pull out all the loose hairs that regularly appear on the carpets, furniture, clothes, and in the baking. "Oh, how lovely, I see you have a Border Terrier," smiles a dinner guest while waving a piece of pastry with a Border

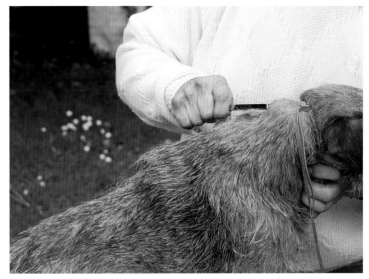

Regular brushing and combing will reduce the amount of Border Terrier hair that is left around the house.

Terrier hair poking out of it.

The best way to groom a Border is with a palm-shaped 'brush' (with an integral backstrap, which fits over your hand so that the comb is snug in your palm). The wire teeth are shaped so that brushing/combing in the direction of the hair growth will tease out old hair and undercoat. A breeder told me many years ago that a redundant hacksaw blade, snapped in half and with a binding 'handle' created at one end, makes a cheap and excellent tool for removing dead hair – and it does.

Border Terriers are not for the house proud. A Border sheds hair constantly, even when recently stripped, and only the introduction of my 'Cat & Dog' vacuum cleaner has managed to keep my home pristine, but, by

bedtime, it's the 'start again' routine. Mine all have quality time with me in the evenings – aside from their walks – and lie on the window seat, the floor and on my lap. Some, in the spirit of enjoyment, wriggle on their backs on the floor, leaving the usual tell-tale hairs everywhere.

Regular brushing helps, but at least twice a year the harsh topcoat begins to 'blow' (i.e. begins to part at the shoulders) and its time to strip. Unless you have a groomer living near to you who fully understands a Border's jacket and how to hand-strip, it's best to learn how to do it yourself.

Joining your nearest Border Terrier club is a good starting point, as events are often held to show people how to strip their dogs.

HAND-STRIPPING

This is a process of pulling out the old coat using finger and thumb. Pet dogs generally need hand-stripping twice a year. Everyone has their own method of hand-stripping. It does not matter where you start, as long as you work methodically.

The coat before hand-stripping

You can use powdered chalk, which makes it easier to get a grip on the hair.

Neck hair should be pulled out following the growth pattern.

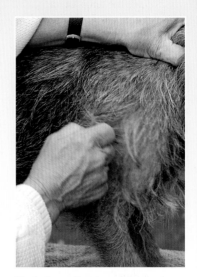

Work down the shoulders.

HAND-STRIPPING

To check if the coat is ready for stripping, take a few long hairs at the shoulders between finger and thumb and pull gently but firmly. If the hair comes away quickly and easily without causing the dog discomfort, it's ready. Then proceed as follows:

- Start at the head above the eyebrows and work backwards. With the dog facing you and with one hand under the chin, take very small amounts of hair and pull backwards in the direction of growth, taking your time.
- Continue this process along the back, sides and down the legs. You will find a stripping comb is helpful on the legs where the hair is very short.
- Neck hair should be pulled out following the growth pattern. You will see between the front legs where the direction of growth changes. Instead of pulling downwards, clean out the gap by pulling upwards.

TRIMMING

When the bulk of the hair is removed, turn the dog away from you and address the tail. Border Terriers traditionally have a light ring of hair about a third of the way down the tail; this is quite normal. The tail shape should resemble that of a carrot, so look at it carefully before you start. The base underneath the tail should be flat and the top round, tapering and carrot-like.
Run your thumb and forefinger down the tail until you feel the end of the tail bone. Using a pair of sharp scissors, keep your thumb over the end of the tail bone and cut around your thumb, using it as a template. Then, gently shake the tail and cut off hanging hairs and side hairs beneath with scissors, working from the tip up to the root. Once complete, pull out any loose hairs around the top of the tail to even the final appearance.

Use your scissors to trim around the feet, cutting out long hair between the pads, but ensuring that the finished foot looks tight and cat-like. Don't cut the hair on top of the foot, otherwise the foot takes on an undesirable flat-footed appearance.

TIDYING

I use scissors to cut off the long sheath hairs protecting a male's penis. It keeps the dog cleaner and stops stale urine smells. Belly hair should also be tidied – but how would you like it if your belly hair was pulled off by   hand?

Ask your Border to lie on his back and cut a 'seam' up the centre of the belly, removing all the long hair. The remaining side hair can be gently removed by hand, a few strands at a time.
Finally, returning to the rear end, comb the hair downwards, and, using your scissors, work downwards, to remove some of the long hair around the anus, trying not to leave visible cut marks in the remaining hair.

NAILS

Claws should wear down naturally with regular road work, except for retained dewclaws. If your dog is sensitive about having his feet pedicured, and, more importantly, if you don't have the correct nail cutters, ask your vet or an experienced friend to do the job for you. One cut, exposing the quick, will mean loss of blood – and a dog who might not let you near his feet again.

EYES AND EARS

Long hairs in and outside the ears should be cleaned out – and remember always to check eyes, ears and beards for cleanliness, not just when stripping twice a year. Sniff inside the ears of your Border regularly. A dog's ears should smell 'doggy' but not unpleasant or 'cheesy'. If the hair inside the ears is kept short, the interior of the outer ear should be visible and clean. If there is a build-up of wax, ask your vet or an experienced breeder to remove it. Do not poke about inside the ear canal, as you may push wax further in. Also, if the dog shakes his head during cleaning, he may harm himself and become reluctant to let you clean his ears again.

The eyes should always be bright and free of discharge in a healthy dog. Any pus or opaque discharge may mean a bout of conjunctivitis, a foreign object in the eye, or a deeper seated problem, such as trouble with the tear duct. Stained hair around the eye from such secretions can be cleaned and dried off with a warm, damp cloth. Left alone, a build-up of hard 'gunk' can form, which, if left, is unsightly and unhealthy. Ask your vet to check the eyes if you are in any doubt.

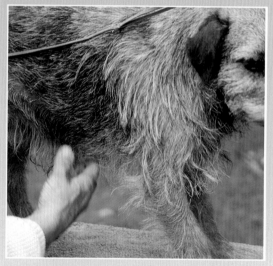

The underside needs to be tidied.

Work down the throat to the chest.

Keep moving down the back and along the body.

The long hair on the hindquarters is pulled out.

The hair underneath the tail is given attention.

The hair above the eyes is pulled out, but making sure the Border Terrier retains a rugged appearance.

Limited trimming will help to tidy up your Border Terrier's appearance. Use scissors to trim the hair around the foot.

THE FINISHED RESULT

A Border Terrier ready to be exhibited in the show ring.

Regular grooming and routine care will ensure that your Border Terrier looks and feels great!

BATHING

A Border Terrier has a weatherproof coat and bathing him removes the natural oils. Unless he has rolled in something truly offensive, which cannot be brushed out, don't bath him. If you must do it, try to choose a warm day. Put cold water in the bath first and then bring it up to a warm temperature – not hot.

Use a shampoo designed for dogs, and take great care when cleaning round his eyes. Make sure all the soap is completely removed before drying your dog and have plenty of towels available – there are never enough!

Once towelled down, brush the coat through and let him run about outside to dry naturally.

PRESENTING A SHOW DOG

There is little difference in presentation and grooming techniques between show Borders and pet Borders. The major and most obvious difference is that the owners of show Borders tend to keep their dogs in show fettle all the time. Coats are kept neat and clean; the dogs are extremely fit, and trimming and tidying is a regular regime. Stripping is carried out regularly, usually twice a year, and emphasis is placed on perfecting technique.

EXERCISE

Regular exercise is essential in order to keep your Border fit, lean and healthy.

FIRST EXERCISE

A nine-week-old puppy, just starting to be trained on a lead, should not be walked any distance. In fact, until all his inoculations are completed, he should remain safely in the garden, away from sites of possible infection where other dogs have fouled and in safe surroundings with siblings, toys or human company to keep him entertained.

By the time a puppy is 12 weeks, he can walk half a mile with no signs of tiredness. Gradually increase his walks; getting him used to his lead, traffic and other pavement users is all part of socialising the puppy (see Chapter Six: Training and Socialisation).

ADULT EXERCISE

Most adult dogs appreciate two walks a day; many get more but some get much less. Borders are undemanding and will be ready to go out whenever you decide to move. They generally love being in a car, as it usually means a trip for a walk somewhere different and exciting. They have no preferences but my own experiences show that they love to be anywhere where sheep or cattle have been – for obvious reasons! They like new things and new places. As dogs with a sense of the ridiculous, I have often played hide-and-seek with mine in woods. They stop to check a smell; I sneak off and hide behind a tree and whistle them up. They may go past you the first time and then enjoy the

A fit Border Terrier thrives on regular and varied exercise.

fun when they realise their mistake, but you will be extremely lucky to catch them out again.

Do you live near water? Some Border Terriers are natural swimmers; others are slower to take to the water. However, don a pair of wellies and with a long stick explore any riverbank and your Border will reward you with enthusiasm, searching out holes, swimming in pools and picking up rubbish.

PLAYTIME WITH A PURPOSE

Stretching your Border Terrier's brain is another essential requisite to keep him healthy. Border Terriers are very sociable dogs and long to please. They have an innate sense of the ridiculous and nothing pleases them more than to join in games. They don't respond well to physical punishment, so to develop the best relationship with your Border, start training and bonding with him as soon as he arrives in your house.

Educate your dog to identify different things and to bring them to you. If they sound phonetically different from one another, a Border will soon 'learn' each object and be delighted to get his task correct and bring the right item to you. It takes time but Border Terriers love the challenge, and it's fun for the owner too. A brush, a ball, a duster – I started my first Border on these items and he was brilliant. I could ask him to bring them to me from another room and he never failed. He loved his games.

Educational toys may sound silly for a dog, but manufacturers realise that dogs are bright and need to be stimulated. Older dogs will enjoy dog blocks – cubes into which titbits are inserted and which rattle. The holes in the cube allow the dog to smell the food and he then has to work out how to get the food out of the cube. In my experience, terriers can solve the problem quickly and then the novelty soon wears off.

CARING FOR AN OLDER DOG

Older dogs beyond the age of 12 should have a lightweight diet, which is formulated towards a more inactive lifestyle. This is the caring age when teeth should be checked regularly; entire bitches

A Border Terrier's needs will change as he grows older.

should be checked for unusual discharges from the vulva, which might suggest an internal infection, and any visible lumps and bumps should be monitored. Feet should be regularly inspected in case of cysts between the toes, and nails that are growing too long through less exercise should be trimmed. Eyes should also be examined regularly for any unusual features developing.

Depending on fitness and any health problems, even a 14-year-old should be able to enjoy a stroll. It's important, as your Border grows older, that you check that he can eat properly and that he has no teeth or gum

disorders – canine dental work can be very expensive.

Borders can live until they are 16 plus, and seldom slow down dramatically until into their mid teens. The introduction of a younger dog frequently rejuvenates an older Border. Old dogs sleep a great deal more and they may have aches and pains. However, there are supplements to help creaking bones and to give pain-free days.

SAYING GOODBYE

The time is never right to say goodbye to a loved Border. We never want a dog to leave us and it doesn't matter how many Borders we have over the years, each is very special and each parting is heartbreaking, whether through an illness, an accident or from old age.

Always make provision for your Border. Should anything happen to you – who will take care of your dog? Have you arranged with a relative to take him? Have you discussed his needs with a friend or family member? Have you thought about adding his care into your will? Many people who retire like an active, smaller dog to enjoy their days and their outings, and these companions are not only devoted, but hold a special place in a person's heart. But an older person must not forget that their Border friend might outlive them – so please consider this.

It is only right that our dogs should die with dignity. If we have given a dog a good and happy life, we can ask no more of our conscience. When talking to a noted breeder many years ago, she declared that "we sometimes keep dogs alive for ourselves, selfishly" – and she is right. The procedures for euthanasia are painless and effective, and how much kinder to allow a loved Border to slip away in comfort and without pain, than struggle on for months, being given medication and with no quality of life?

It is the hardest thing to say goodbye, and those of us who love our dogs will always find it difficult to let go. But our dogs cannot tell us when they are in pain; we have to make that judgement call. Most people who cherish their dogs will know when the time is right – they 'read' their dogs and they know.

A Border is a character and always remains so. Sixteen years of life is a long time – a Border bought for a child may still be around for that child's babies, which is why they mean so much – they have seen so much and experienced so much. The next puppy will help to heal the loss, but it will be different. They all are, which is why we keep them.

SUMMING UP

A Border Terrier is a complex bundle of so many things: a soft lapdog, a courageous working dog, an active sporting dog, a good tracker, and a great soulmate. He listens, he learns and he loves. He doesn't always obey – but that's a Border Terrier!

There is something very special about the companionship of an older dog.

TRAINING AND SOCIALISATION

Chapter 6

When you decided to bring a Border Terrier into your life, you probably had dreams of how it was going to be: long walks together, cosy evenings with a Border lying devotedly at your feet, and whenever you returned home, there would always be a special welcome waiting for you.

There is no doubt that you can achieve all this – and much more – with a Border Terrier, but like anything that is worth having, you must be prepared to put in the work. A Border Terrier, regardless of whether it is a puppy or an adult, does not come ready trained, understanding exactly what you want and fitting perfectly into your lifestyle. A Border Terrier has to learn his place in your family and he must discover what is acceptable behaviour.

We have a great starting point in that the Border Terrier has an outstanding temperament. Most Border Terrier owners would agree that the Border is more sensitive than the other terrier breeds. Although he was bred to go to earth, and therefore shows courage and initiative, he also had to work alongside other dogs, which has made him more easy-going. When underground, a Border Terrier had to think for himself in order to survive, and so he may not be as tuned into his handler as gundog or herding breeds, but it is all a matter of knowing which buttons to press in order to get the best from your dog.

THE FAMILY PACK

Dogs have been domesticated for some 14,000 years and so their links to their distant ancestor, the wolf, have become increasingly diluted. The Border Terrier was bred to follow horsemen, and when an earth was discovered, it was his job to dislodge the fox. The instinct to hunt, and the courage and tenacity needed to take on a fox made him an exceptional working dog – but these virtues are not sought after in pet dogs. The survival skills needed in the wild are equally redundant in the domesticated dog who is provided with all he needs in terms of food and shelter.

However, there are some useful parallels to draw between the Border Terrier who lives in your home, and the wild wolf who must hunt and kill in order to survive. The wolf's success as a species relies on living in a pack, co-operating with fellow pack members in order to hunt, to ward off danger, to find shelter, to breed, and to rear young. The domesticated dog joins the family circle and he, too, needs to co-operate with his fellow pack members. In much the same way as a wolf, he needs food, shelter and companionship, and he also needs someone who will make the important decisions.

In a world of domesticated dogs, there is no need to think of yourself as the 'pack leader'; it has little relevance to modern life and it also has negative connotations as it suggests that you are a god-like figure in absolute authority. It is more useful to think of yourself as a mentor, helping and guiding your dog to make the right decisions.

Have you got what it takes to be a kind and caring mentor?

ESTABLISHING RESPECT

In order to live in harmony, a sense of mutual respect must be established among pack/family members. There needs to be clarity as to who is the decision-maker, and a reason why decisions are accepted. Problems occur if lines are blurred and there is a constant juggling for positions.

When a Border Terrier arrives in your home, you need to establish yourself as a kind, caring, consistent mentor, rewarding the behaviour you want so your pup always has a reason to co-operate.

There are a number of guidelines which will help you to establish mutual respect:

- **Keep it simple:** Decide on the rules you want your Border Terrier to obey and always make it 100 per cent clear what is acceptable, and what is unacceptable, behaviour.
- **Be consistent:** If you are not consistent about enforcing rules, how can you expect your Border Terrier to take you seriously? There is nothing worse than allowing your Border to jump up on to the sofa one moment and then scolding him the next time he does it because he is muddy. As far as the Border Terrier is concerned, he may as well try it on because he can't predict your reaction.
- **Get your timing right:** If are rewarding your Border Terrier,

marking the behaviour you want, you need to be spot-on with your timing. You need to respond within one or two seconds otherwise he will not link his behaviour with your reaction (see page 96).

- **Read your dog's body language:** Find out how to read body language and facial expressions (see page 93) so that you understand your Border Terrier's feelings and his intentions.
- **Be aware of your own body language:** The Border Terrier is a relatively small dog, and your upright figure may appear intimidating. Equally, if you over-shadow your dog, he may feel pressurised. Try working alongside your dog rather than directly in front of him, and when you have a game, why not get down on his level so you can interact as equal partners?
- **Tone of voice:** Dogs are receptive to tone of voice, so you can use your voice to praise him or to correct undesirable behaviour. If you are pleased with your Border Terrier, praise him to the skies in a warm, happy voice. If you want to stop him raiding the bin, use a deep, firm voice when you say "No".
- **Give one command only:** If

you keep repeating a command, or keep changing it, your Border Terrier will think you are babbling and will probably ignore you. If your Border does not respond the first time you ask, make it simple by using a treat to lure him into position, and then you can reward him for a correct response.

- **Daily reminders:** A young, exuberant Border Terrier is apt to forget his manners from time to time, and an adolescent dog may attempt to challenge your authority (see page 107). Rather than coming down on your Border Terrier like a ton of bricks when he does something wrong, try to prevent bad manners by daily reminders of good manners. For example:

i   Do not let your dog barge ahead of you when you are going through a door.

ii Do not let him leap out of the car the moment you open the door (which could be potentially lethal, as well as being disrespectful).

iii Do not let him eat from your hand when you are at the table.

iv If you playing a game with your Border Terrier, do not allow him to dictate proceedings. You start the game, and you end it, rather than allowing him to run off with the toy. Make sure you swap the toy for a treat so your Border Terrier has a good reason to co-operate.

Be consistent in your training: if your Border Terrier is not allowed on the sofa, make sure he never breaks this rule.

UNDERSTANDING YOUR BORDER TERRIER

Body language is an important means of communication between dogs, which they use to make friends, to assert status, and to avoid conflict. It is important to get on your dog's wavelength by understanding his body language and reading his facial expressions. Behaviourists have made detailed studies of canine body language; it is a complex subject that is beyond the scope of this book. However, it is useful to look at some of the basic forms of communication:

- A positive body posture and a wagging tail indicate a happy, confident dog.
- A crouched body posture with ears back and tail down show

that a dog is being submissive. A dog may do this when he is being told off or if a more assertive dog approaches him.

- A bold dog will stand tall, looking strong and alert. His ears will be forward and his tail will be held high.
- A dog who raises his hackles (lifting the fur along his topline) is trying to look as scary as possible. This may be the prelude to aggressive behaviour, but, in many cases, the dog is apprehensive and is unsure how to cope with a situation.
- A playful dog will go down on his front legs while standing on his hind legs in a bow position. This friendly invitation says: "I'm no threat, let's play."
- An assertive, aggressive dog will meet other dogs with a hard

CANINE BODY LANGUAGE

This dog (facing) is confident and assertive as he meets a more submissive dog.

The younger dog (left) has opted for complete submission, telling the other dog that he presents no threat.

stare. If he is challenged, he may bare his teeth and growl, and the corners of his mouth will be drawn forward. His ears will be forward and he will appear tense in every muscle.

- A nervous dog will often show aggressive behaviour as a means of self-protection. If threatened, this dog will lower his head and flatten his ears. The corners of his mouth may be drawn back, and he may bark or whine.
- The Border Terrier has a unique way of showing his displeasure. He will sink his neck into his body, and his tail will go down, giving a very good imitation of an angry hedgehog. If your Border Terrier gets the hump, he will go into a sulk and wait for you to 'win' him round…

CALMING SIGNALS

These are signals that are used between dogs to communicate unease or discomfort, and they will generally put a stop to potential situations of conflict. Dogs try to use this system to communicate with us, and our inability to read these signals can be the cause of stress and misunderstanding.

There are at least 30 recognised calming signals, and your dog will have his own individual repertoire. Some of the more common, and obvious, signals include:

- Licking/tongue flicks
- Blinking
- Yawning
- Head turns
- Walking in a curve
- Sniffing

Your dog may use calming signals to communicate his concern in the following situations:

- When he is being hugged or kissed
- If someone maintains eye contact for a prolonged period
- When there are raised voices and quarrelling in the family
- When he doesn't understand a training exercise, or when a training session has gone on for too long
- When he has to put up with something he dislikes, e.g. nail trimming
- When he feels trapped

If you see any of these signs, try to moderate your behaviour to make life easier for your Border Terrier. If you are observant you

GIVING REWARDS

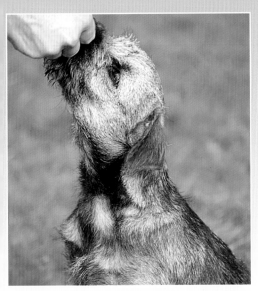

Initially, a Border puppy will be more easily trained with food treats.

If you work at playing with your Border, he will be motivated by a toy.

will, over time, become expert at understanding his feelings and therefore reducing potential stress and anxiety.

GIVING REWARDS

Why should your Border Terrier do as you ask? If you follow the guidelines given above, your Border Terrier should respect your authority, but what about the time when he sees a squirrel that he wants to chase or has found a really enticing scent? The answer is that you must always be the most interesting, the most attractive, and the most irresistible person in your Border Terrier's eyes. It would be nice to think you could achieve this by personality alone, but most of us need a little extra help.

You need to find out what is the biggest reward for your dog. In a Border Terrier's case, it will nearly always be food. Known as a stomach on legs, the Border Terrier is highly motivated by food treats, and will give you his full attention when you have something tasty to give him. A Border Terrier is also motivated by toys – particularly tuggies or a ball on a rope – but you need to start playing with your Border Terrier when he is young, and maintain play sessions throughout his adult life in order to fuel his enthusiasm. A game with a toy or working for food treats are equally effective, as long as you are giving your dog something he really wants.

When you are teaching a dog a new exercise, you should reward your Border Terrier frequently.

When he knows the exercise or command, reward him randomly so that he keeps on responding to you in a positive manner. If your dog does something extra special, like leaving a scent and running back to you on command, make sure he really knows how pleased you are by giving him a handful of treats or throwing his ball a few extra times. If he gets a bonanza reward, he is more likely to come back on future occasions, because you have proved to be even more rewarding than his previous activity.

TOP TREATS

Some trainers grade treats depending on what they are asking the dog to do. A dog may get a low-grade treat, such as a piece of dry food, to reward good

Reinforce the behaviour you want by rewarding it, and then your Border Terrier has a good reason to repeat it.

behaviour on a random basis, such as sitting when you open a door or allowing you to examine his teeth. But high-grade treats, which may be cooked liver, sausage or cheese, are reserved for training new exercises or for use in the park when you want a really good recall. Whatever type of treat you use, remember to subtract it from your Border Terrier's daily ration. Fat dogs are lethargic, prone to health problems, and will almost certainly have a shorter life expectancy. Reward your Border Terrier, but always keep a check on his figure!

HOW DO DOGS LEARN?

It is not difficult to get inside your Border Terrier's head and understand how he learns, as it is not dissimilar to the way we learn. Dogs learn by conditioning: they find out that specific behaviours produce specific consequences. This is known as operant conditioning or consequence learning. Consequences have to be immediate or clearly linked to the behaviour, as a dog sees the world in terms of action and result. Dogs will quickly learn if an action has a bad consequence or a good consequence.

Dogs also learn by association. This is known as classical conditioning or association learning. It is the type of learning made famous by Pavlov's experiment with dogs. Pavlov presented dogs with food and measured their salivary response (how much they drooled). Then he rang a bell just before presenting the food. At first, the dogs did not salivate until the food was presented. But after a while they learnt that the sound of the bell meant that food was coming, and so they salivated when they heard the bell. A dog needs to learn the association in

THE CLICKER REVOLUTION

Karen Pryor pioneered the technique of clicker training when she was working with dolphins. Karen wanted to mark 'correct' behaviour at the precise moment it happened. She found it was impossible to toss a fish to a dolphin when it was in mid-air, when she wanted to reward it. Her aim was to establish a conditioned response so the dolphin knew that it had performed correctly and a reward would follow.

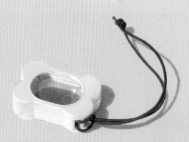

The solution was the clicker: a small matchbox-shaped training aid, with a metal tongue that makes a click when it is pressed. To begin with, the dolphin had to learn that a click meant that food was coming. The dolphin then learnt that it must 'earn' a click in order to get a reward. Clicker training has been used with many different animals, most particularly with dogs, and it has proved hugely successful. Many trainers have noted that Border Terriers, who are quick to learn and like taking the initiative, respond extremely well to clicker training.

order for it to have any meaning. For example, a dog that has never seen a lead before will be completely indifferent to it. A dog that has learnt that a lead means he is going for a walk will get excited the second he sees the lead; he has learnt to associate a lead with a walk.

BE POSITIVE

The most effective method of training dogs is to use their ability to learn by consequence and to teach that the behaviour you want produces a good consequence. For example, if you ask your Border Terrier to "Sit" and reward him with a treat, he will learn that it is worth his while to sit on command because it will lead to a reward. He is more likely to repeat the behaviour, and the behaviour will become stronger, because it results in a positive outcome. This method of training, known as positive reinforcement, generally leads to a happy, co-operative dog that is willing to work, and a handler who has fun training their dog.

The opposite approach is negative reinforcement. This is far less effective and often results in a poor relationship between dog and owner. In this method of training, you ask your Border Terrier to "Sit", and, if he does not respond, you deliver a sharp yank on the training collar or push his rear to the ground. The dog learns that not responding to your command has a bad consequence, and he may be less likely to ignore you in the future. However, it may well have a bad consequence for you, too. A dog that is treated in this way may associate harsh handling with the handler and become aggressive or fearful. Instead of establishing a pattern of willing co-operation, you are establishing a relationship built on coercion.

It will not take your Border Terrier long to learn that he must 'earn' a click in order to get a reward.

GETTING STARTED

When you train your Border Terrier, you will develop your own techniques as you get to know what motivates him.

You may decide to get involved with clicker training or you may prefer to go for a simple command-and-reward formula. It does not matter what form of training you use, as long as it is based on positive, reward-based methods.

There are a few important guidelines to bear in mind when you are training your Border Terrier:

- Find a training area that is free from distractions, particularly when you are just starting out. A Border Terrier loves to use his nose, and so it is important to keep his attention focused on you. To begin with, train your puppy in the house where there will not be so many enticing smells. You can also attempt to find an area, such as a deserted car park or a tennis court, which has a hard surface and will prove less distracting.

- Keep training sessions short, especially with young puppies that have very short attention spans.

- Make training sessions fun so that your Border Terrier wants to work for you. If you turn training into a military drill, your Border Terrier will switch off because he finds it dull and repetitive. Training should be one big game, interspersed with lots of treats and plenty of praise.

- Do not train if you are in a bad mood or if you are on a tight schedule – the training session will be doomed to failure.
- If you are using a toy as a reward, make sure it is only available when you are training. In this way it has an added value.
- If you are using food treats, make sure they are bite-size and easy to swallow; you don't want to hang about while your dog chews on his treat.
- All food treats must be deducted from your Border's daily food ration.
- Remember that dogs do not generalise, so when you have taught your Border Terrier an exercise you will need to take it to different places to cement his learning.
- If your Border Terrier is finding an exercise difficult, try not to get frustrated. Go back a step and praise him for his effort. You will probably find he is more successful when you try again at the next training session.
- Break exercises down to their component parts. Back chain if possible, which means teaching an exercise in the reverse order, especially with more complex exercises, such as the retrieve.
- Always end training sessions on a happy, positive note. Ask your Border Terrier to do something you know he can do – it could be a trick he enjoys performing – and then reward him with a few treats or an extra-long play session.

THE X FACTOR

There are times when you want to reward good behaviour with a click – but you do not have a clicker to hand. To get round this, you can teach your Border Terrier a clicker 'word', which you can use instead. Make sure the word you use bears no resemblance to any other words you use when 'talking' to your dog, either when you are training him, playing with him, or simply interacting with him on walks or around the home, otherwise the clicker word will lose its value as a specific marker of desirable behaviour. A number of trainers use 'X' as their clicker word – and dogs seem to respond well to this. The great advantage of having a clicker word is that you can use it in competition when you would not be able to use a clicker.

In the exercises that follow, clicker training is introduced and followed, but all the exercises will work without the use of a clicker.

INTRODUCING A CLICKER

This is dead easy, and your ever-hungry Border Terrier will learn about the clicker in record time! It can be combined with attention training, which is a very useful tool and can be used on many different occasions.

- Prepare some treats and go to an area that is free from distractions. When your Border Terrier stops sniffing around and looks at you, click and reward by throwing him a treat. This means he will not crowd you, but will go looking for the treat. Repeat a couple of times. If your dog is very easily distracted, you may need to start this exercise with the dog on a lead.
- After a few clicks, your Border Terrier understands that if he hears a click, he will get a treat. He must now learn that he must 'earn' a click. This time, when your Border Terrier looks at you, wait a little longer before clicking, and then reward him. If your dog is on a lead but responding well, try him off the lead.
- When your Border Terrier is working for a click and giving you his attention, you can introduce a cue or command word, such as "Watch". Repeat a few times, using the cue. You now have a dog that understands the clicker and will give you his attention when you ask him to "Watch".

TRAINING EXERCISES

THE SIT

This is the easiest exercise to teach, so it is rewarding for both you and your Border Terrier.

- Choose a tasty treat and hold it just above your puppy's nose. As he looks up at the treat, he will naturally go into the Sit. As soon as he is in position, reward him
- Repeat the exercise, and when your pup understands what you want, introduce the "Sit" command.
- You can practise at mealtimes by holding out the bowl and waiting for your dog to sit. Most Borders learn this one very quickly!

THE DOWN

Work hard at this exercise because a reliable Down is useful in many different situations, and an instant Down can be a lifesaver (see Chasing, page110).

- You can start with your dog in a Sit, or it is just as effective to teach it when the dog is standing. Hold a treat just below your puppy's nose, and slowly lower it towards the ground. The treat acts as a lure, and your puppy will follow it, first going down on his forequarters, and then bringing his hindquarters down as he tries to get the treat.

As you lower a treat to the ground, your puppy will follow it and go into a Down. You can apply gentle pressure on the shoulders to help him maintain the position for a few seconds.

- Make sure you close your fist around the treat, and only reward your puppy with the treat when he is in the correct position. If your puppy is reluctant to go Down, you can apply gentle pressure on his shoulders to encourage him to go into the correct position.
- When your puppy is following the treat and going in to position, introduce a verbal command.
- Build up this exercise over a period of time, each time waiting a little longer before giving the reward, so the puppy learns to stay in the Down position.

THE RECALL

With a Border Terrier, it is never too soon to start training the Recall. This is a breed that loves nothing more than following a scent, and a Border is famous for becoming deaf to all calls when he has picked up an enticing trail. Make sure you are always happy and excited when your Border Terrier comes to you, even if he has been slower than you would like. Your dog must believe that the greatest reward is coming to you.

- You can start teaching the Recall from the moment your puppy arrives home. He will naturally follow you, so keep calling his name and rewarding him when he comes to you.
- Practise in the garden, and, when your puppy is busy exploring, get his attention by calling his name. As he runs towards you, introduce the verbal command "Come". Make sure you sound exciting, so your puppy wants to come to you. When he responds, give him lots of praise.
- If your puppy is slow to respond, try running away a few paces or jumping up and down. It doesn't matter how silly you look – the key issue is to get your puppy's attention and then make yourself irresistible!
- In a dog's mind, coming when called should be regarded as the best fun because he knows he is always going to be

Build up an enthusiastic response to the Recall.

SECRET WEAPON

You can build up a strong Recall by using another form of association learning. Buy a whistle, and when you are giving your Border Terrier his food, peep on the whistle. You can choose the type of signal you want to give: two short peeps or one long whistle, for example. Within a matter of days, your dog will learn that the sound of the whistle means that food is coming.

Now transfer the lesson outside. Arm yourself with some tasty treats and the whistle. Allow your Border Terrier to run free in the garden, and, after a couple of minutes, use the whistle. The dog has already learnt to associate the whistle with food, so he will come towards you.

Immediately reward him with a treat and lots of praise. Repeat the lesson a few times in the garden so you are confident that your dog is responding before trying it in the park. Make sure you always have some treats in your pocket when you go for a walk, and your dog will quickly learn how rewarding it is to come to you.

rewarded. Never make the mistake of telling your dog off, no matter how slow he is to respond, as you will undo all your previous hard work.

- When you are free-running your dog, make sure you have his favourite toy or a pocket full of treats, so you can reward him at intervals throughout the walk when you call him to you. Do not allow your dog to free-run and only call him back at the end of the walk to clip on his lead. An intelligent Border Terrier will soon realise that the Recall means the end of his walk, and then end of fun – so who can blame him for not wanting to come back?

Be quick to reward as soon as your puppy comes to you.

TRAINING LINE

This is the equivalent of a very long lead, which you can buy at a pet store, or you can make your own with a length of rope. The training line is attached to your Border Terrier's collar and should be around 15 feet (4.5 metres) in length.

The purpose of the training line is to prevent your dog from disobeying you so that he never has the chance to get into bad habits. For example, when you call your Border Terrier and he ignores you, you can immediately pick up the end of the training line and call him again. By picking up the line, you will have attracted his attention, and if you call in an excited, happy voice, your Border Terrier will come to you. The moment he does so, give him a tasty treat so he is instantly rewarded for making the 'right' decision.

The training line is very useful when your Border Terrier becomes an adolescent and is testing your leadership. When you have reinforced the correct behaviour a number of times, your dog will build up a strong Recall and you will not need to use a training line.

WALKING ON A LOOSE LEAD

This is a simple exercise, but if you do not work on it, you will end up with a dog who pulls on the lead – and on-lead walks will be a chore. In most cases, owners are too impatient, wanting to get on with the expedition rather that training the dog how to walk on a lead.

- In the early stages of lead training, allow your puppy to pick his route and follow him. He will get used to the feeling of being 'attached' to you, and has no reason to put up any resistance.
- Next, find a toy or a tasty treat and show it to your puppy. Let him follow the treat/toy for a few paces, and then reward him.
- Build up the amount of time your pup will walk with you, and when he is walking nicely

LEAD TRAINING

A puppy may resist walking on a lead to begin with.

Give plenty of praise and encouragement so your puppy is keen to walk with you.

by your side, introduce the verbal command "Heel" or "Close". Give lots of praise when your pup is in the correct position.

- When your pup is walking alongside you, keep focusing his attention on you by using his name or the "Watch" command, and then rewarding him when he looks at you. If it is going well, introduce some changes of direction.
- Do not attempt to take your puppy out on the lead until you have mastered the basics at home. You need to be confident that your puppy accepts the lead and will focus

his attention on you, when requested, before you face the challenge of a busy environment.

- As your Border Terrier gets older, he may try to pull on the lead, particularly if you are heading somewhere he wants to go, such as the park. If this happens, stop, call your dog to you, and do not set off again until he is in the correct position. If necessary, walk a few paces in the opposite direction so that he learns that pulling does not get him to the desired destination any quicker. It may take time, but your Border Terrier will

eventually realise that it is more productive to walk by your side than to pull ahead.

STAYS

This may not be the most exciting exercise, but it is one of the most useful. There are many occasions when you want your Border Terrier to stay in position, even if it is only for a few seconds. The classic example is when you want your dog to stay in the back of the car until you have clipped on his lead.

Some trainers use the verbal command "Stay" when the dog is to stay in position for an extended period of time, and

Build up the Stay exercise in easy stages.

"Wait" if the dog is to stay in position for a few seconds until you give the next command. Others trainers use a universal "Stay" to cover all situations. It all comes down to personal preference, and as long as you are consistent, your dog will understand the command he is given. If you have a lively pup, you may find it easier to train this exercise on the lead.

• Put your puppy in a Sit or a Down, and use a hand signal (flat palm, facing the dog) to show he is to stay in position. Step a pace away from the dog. Wait a second, step back and reward him. You may find it easier to take a step to the side, as your puppy is less likely to follow you. Repeat the exercise, gradually increasing the distance you can leave your dog. When you return to your dog's side, praise him quietly, and release him with a command, such as "OK".

• Remember to keep your body language very still when you are training this exercise, and avoid eye contact with your dog. Work on this exercise over a period of time, and you will build up a really reliable Stay.

SOCIALISATION

While your Border Terrier is mastering basic obedience

exercises, there is other, equally important, work to do with him. A Border Terrier is not only becoming a part of your home and family, he is becoming a member of the community. He needs to be able to live in the outside world, coping calmly with every new situation that comes his way. It is your job to introduce him to as many different experiences as possible, and encourage him to behave in an appropriate manner.

In order to socialise your Border Terrier effectively, it is helpful to understand how his brain is developing, and then you will get a perspective on how he sees the world.

CANINE SOCIALISATION (Birth to 7 weeks)

This is the time when a dog learns how to be a dog. By interacting with his mother and his littermates, a young pup learns about leadership and submission. He learns to read body posture so that he understands the intentions of his mother and his siblings. A puppy that is taken away from his litter too early may always have behavioural problems with other dogs, either being fearful or aggressive.

SOCIALISATION PERIOD (7 to 12 weeks)

This is the time to get cracking and introduce your puppy to as many different experiences as possible. This includes meeting different people, other dogs and animals, seeing new sights, and hearing a range of sounds, from the vacuum cleaner to the roar of traffic. At this stage, a puppy learns very quickly and what he learns will stay with him for the rest of his life. This is the best time for a puppy to move to a new home, as he is adaptable and ready to form deep bonds.

FEAR-IMPRINT PERIOD (8 to 11 weeks)

This occurs during the socialisation period, and it can be the cause of problems if it is not handled carefully. If a pup is exposed to a frightening or painful experience, it will lead to lasting impressions. Obviously, you will attempt to avoid frightening situations, such as your pup being bullied by a mean-spirited older dog, or a firework going off, but you cannot always protect your puppy from the unexpected. If your pup has a nasty experience, the best plan is to make light of it and distract him by offering him a treat or a game. The pup will take the lead from you and will be reassured that there is nothing to worry about. If you mollycoddle him and sympathise with him, he is far more likely to retain the memory of his fear.

SENIORITY PERIOD (12 to 16 weeks)

During this period, your Border Terrier starts to cut the apron strings and becomes more independent. He will test out his status to find out who is the pack leader: him or you. Bad habits, such as play biting, which may

have been seen as endearing a few weeks earlier, should be firmly discouraged. Remember to use positive, reward-based training, but make sure your puppy knows that you are the leader and must be respected.

SECOND FEAR-IMPRINT PERIOD (6 to 14 months)

This period is not as critical as the first fear-imprint period, but it should still be handled carefully. During this time your Border Terrier may appear apprehensive,

A young puppy soaks up new experiences like a sponge.

or he may show fear of something familiar. You may feel as if you have taken a backwards step, but if you adopt a calm, positive manner, your dog will see that there is nothing to be frightened of. Do not make your dog confront the thing that frightens him. Simply distract his attention and give him something else to think about, such as obeying a simple command, such as "Sit" or "Down". This will give you the opportunity to praise and reward your dog, and it will help to boost his confidence.

Make sure your Border Terrier gets out and about so that he takes all new situations in his stride.

YOUNG ADULTHOOD AND MATURITY (1 to 4 years)

The timing of this phase depends on the size of the dog: the bigger the dog, the later it is. This period coincides with a dog's increased size and strength, mental as well as physical. Some dogs, particularly those with a dominant nature, will test your leadership again and may become aggressive towards other dogs. Firmness and continued training are essential at this time so that your Border Terrier accepts his status in the family pack.

IDEAS FOR SOCIALISATION

When you are socialising your Border Terrier, you want him to experience as many different situations as possible. Try out some of the following ideas, which will ensure your Border Terrier has an all-round education.

If you are taking on a rescued dog and have little knowledge of his background, it is important to work through a programme of socialisation. A young puppy soaks up new experiences like a sponge, but an older dog can still learn. If a rescued dog shows fear or apprehension, treat him in exactly the same way as you would treat a youngster who is going through the second fear-imprint period (see earlier).

• Accustom your puppy to household noises, such as the vacuum cleaner, the television and the washing machine.
• Ask visitors to come to the door, wearing different types of clothing – for example, wearing a hat, a long raincoat, or carrying a stick or an umbrella.
• If you do not have children at home, make sure your Border Terrier has a chance to meet and play with them. Go to a local park and watch children in the play area. You will not be able to take your dog inside the play area, but he will see children playing and will get used to their shouts of excitement.
• Attend puppy classes. These are designed for puppies between the ages of 12 to 20 weeks, and give puppies a chance to play and interact together in a controlled, supervised environment. This is particularly important for a Border Terrier, who needs to meet well-mannered dogs of a similar age. Borders get on

TRAINING CLUBS

There are lots of training clubs to choose from. Your vet will probably have details of clubs in your area, or you can ask friends who have dogs if they attend a club. Alternatively, use the internet to find out more information. But how do you know if the club is any good?

Before you take your dog, ask if you can go to a class as an observer and find out the following:
• What experience does the instructor(s) have?
• Do they have experience with Border Terriers?
• Is the class well organised, and are the dogs reasonably quiet? (A noisy class indicates an unruly atmosphere, which will not be conducive to learning.)
• Are there are a number of classes to suit dogs of different ages and abilities?
• Are positive, reward-based training methods used?
• Does the club train for the Good Citizen Scheme? (see page 115)

If you are not happy with the training club, find another one. An inexperienced instructor who cannot handle a number of dogs in a confined environment can do more harm than good.

well with other dogs – particularly bigger dogs – but if they are exposed to aggressive or unpredictable dogs on a few occasions, they may well become pro-active. Unfortunately, this could have a lasting effect on subsequent interactions with other dogs.
• Take a walk around some quiet streets, such as a residential area, so your Border Terrier can get used to the sound of traffic. As he becomes more confident, progress to busier areas.
• Go to a railway station. You don't have to get on a train if you don't need to, but your Border Terrier will have the chance to experience trains, people wheeling luggage, loudspeaker announcements, and going up and down stairs and over railway bridges.
• If you live in the town, plan a trip to the country. You can enjoy a day out and provide an opportunity for your order terrier to see livestock, such as sheep, cattle and horses, in a controlled situation.
• One of the best places for socialising a dog is at a country fair. There will be crowds of people, livestock in pens, tractors, bouncy castles, fairground rides and food stalls.
• When your dog is over 20 weeks of age, find a training class for adult dogs. You may find that your local training class has both puppy and adult classes.

THE ADOLESCENT BORDER TERRIER
It happens to every dog – and every owner. One minute you have an obedient well-behaved youngster, and the next you have an adolescent who appears to have forgotten everything he learnt. This applies equally to males and females, although the type of adolescent behaviour, and its onset, varies between individuals.

Small breeds tend to reach adolescence earlier than larger breeds. In most cases a Border Terrier male will be sexually

When a Border Terrier hits adolescence he may start to test the boundaries.

mature at around five months, and you can expect behavioural changes for at least a couple of months. In most cases, a male Border Terrier will not change dramatically in personality at this time. But he may be less biddable; it is almost as if he's saying: "I'm grown up now – I don't need to come to you or to do as I'm told."

Female Border Terriers show adolescent behaviour as they approach their first season, which is usually between five and seven months of age. At this time, a female Border Terrier may be moody, but she is rarely stroppy. Some bitches may also be a little more clingy. In order to cope with adolescent behaviour, try to see the world from your Border Terrier's perspective.

Just like a teenager, an adolescent Border feels the need to flex his muscles and challenge the status quo. He may become disobedient and break house rules as he tests your authority and your role as leader. Your response must be firm, fair and consistent. Try to avoid confrontations, and be quick to reward good behaviour so that your Border Terrier finds that fitting in with his family is more rewarding than making up his own agenda.

WHEN THINGS GO WRONG

Positive, reward-based training has proved to be the most effective method of teaching dogs, but what happens when your Border Terrier does something wrong and you need to show him that his behaviour is unacceptable? The old-fashioned school of dog training used to rely on the powers of punishment and negative reinforcement. A dog who raided the bin, for example, was smacked. Now we have learnt that it is not only unpleasant and cruel to hit a dog, it is also ineffective. If you hit a dog for stealing, he is more than likely to see you as the bad consequence of stealing, so he may raid the bin again, but probably not when you are around. If he raided the bin some time before you discovered it, he will be even more confused by your punishment, as he will not relate your response to his 'crime'.

A more commonplace example is when a dog fails to respond to a Recall in the park. When the dog eventually comes back, the owner puts the dog on the lead and goes straight home to punish the dog for his poor response. Unfortunately, the dog will have a different interpretation. He does not think: "I won't ignore a Recall command because the bad consequence is the end of my play in the park." He thinks: "Coming to my owner resulted in the end of playtime – therefore coming to my owner has a bad consequence, so I won't do that again."

There are a number of strategies to tackle undesirable behaviour – and they have nothing to do with harsh handling.

Ignoring bad behaviour: The Border Terrier loves to be involved in everything that is going on, but this can lead to attention-seeking behaviour, such as jumping up. As the Border is only a small dog, it is all too easy to ignore jumping up until it becomes an ingrained habit that is difficult to break. But you do have an effective weapon: if your dog is demanding attention, ignore him.

When he jumps up, do not look at him, do not speak to him, and do not push him down – all these actions are rewarding for him. But someone who turns their back on him and offers no response is plain boring. The moment your Border Terrier has four feet on the ground, give him lots of praise and maybe a treat.

If you repeat this often enough, your Border Terrier will learn that jumping up does not have any good consequences, such as getting attention. Instead he is ignored. However, when he has all four feet on the ground, he gets loads of attention. He links the action with the consequence and chooses the action that is most rewarding.

You will find that this strategy works well with all attention-seeking behaviour, such as barking (see page 109), whining or scrabbling at doors. Being ignored is a worst-case scenario for a Border Terrier, so remember to use it as an effective training tool.

PROBLEM BEHAVIOUR

If you have trained your Border Terrier from puppyhood, survived his adolescence and established yourself as a kind and caring mentor, you will end up with a brilliant companion dog. The Border Terrier is a well-balanced dog who is easy-going and biddable, and rarely has hang-ups. The Border Terrier asks for nothing more than to spend time with his beloved family.

However, problems may arise unexpectedly, or you may have taken on a rescued Border Terrier that has established behavioural problems. If you are worried about your dog and feel out of your depth, do not delay in seeking professional help. This is readily available, usually through a referral from your vet, or you can find out additional

Jumping up is one of the most common forms of attention-seeking behaviour.

information on the internet. An animal behaviourist will have experience in tackling problem behaviour and will be able to help both you and your dog.

BARKING

The small terrier breeds tend to be vocal, and the Border Terrier is no exception. A warning bark when your dog hears a strange sound or when the doorbell rings is acceptable. But a dog who barks continuously is a pain for you – and your neighbours – to live with.

The most common scenario is for a dog to start barking, and you respond by shouting at him, telling him to be quiet. The dog does not understand that you are telling him to stop barking; he sees he is getting lots of attention when he barks, so there is no reason to stop. He gets excited by all the noise, and barks louder so that he can have his say! This situation can often be exacerbated when there are young children in the family who have not been taught how to behave with a dog. The children run riot, the parents shout – and the Border Terrier gets hyped up and joins in the general din.

There are a number of steps to take to prevent excessive barking:

It won't take long for your Border Terrier to learn that he gets attention when he calm and quiet.

- Do not shout at your dog when he barks, but distract his attention by bringing out his favourite toy or offering him a treat. As soon as you have his attention and he stops barking, say "Quiet" and click and treat or use the "X" clicker word and treat. Repeat this on as many occasions as possible so that your dog learns that the reward comes when he is "Quiet".

- Do not put your Border Terrier in situations where he is likely to bark and get into the habit of continuous barking. For example, if there are children playing noisy games in the garden, put your Border Terrier in his crate rather than letting him get over-excited. Some Border Terriers love to bark at passers-by, and if you see signs of your Border Terrier doing this, keep him away from the places where he can stand sentry and bark. If you allow a Border Terrier to sit by the window and bark at every sight and every sound, he will be more than happy to oblige – and you can only blame yourself for letting him become a thorough nuisance.

CHASING

The Border Terrier has a strong instinct to chase, and, unlike other breeds, he will go in for the kill. This behaviour may be acceptable for a dog who lives on a farm and is getting rid of mice and rats, but when a pet Border Terrier turns his attention to the neighbourhood cats, it is quite another matter.

How can you stop your Border Terrier chasing? Most importantly, do not encourage behaviour that is likely to stimulate the chasing instinct. If a behaviour driven by instinct is allowed to develop, it will become stronger and stronger – and soon you will have a Border Terrier that is beyond your control.

Take the following steps to inhibit and control the chasing instinct:

- Do not focus on throwing balls or kicking footballs for your Border Terrier to chase. It is better to teach your dog to retrieve so that he learns to bring a toy back to you. This gives your Border Terrier a stimulating game to play, and you can reward him for bringing the toy back with a game or a food treat.
- Work on the instant Down (see page 100). If your Border Terrier responds to this command, you can stop him in his tracks.

- Do not let your dog off-lead away from home until you are confident that he will respond to the Recall. It is much better to exercise your Border Terrier on an extending lead than risk him going off in pursuit of a rabbit, a squirrel or a cat.

All dogs are individuals; Border Terriers will exhibit different characteristics depending on their bloodlines. For example, some lines produce a tougher, more challenging type with a very strong prey drive, whereas others will produce a Border Terrier that is almost as soft as a Labrador! It is all a matter of getting to know your Border Terrier and finding a strategy that works for both of you.

RESTORING THE BALANCE.
If you have trained and socialised your Border Terrier correctly, he will become an integral member of the family circle, and will live with you in a spirit of co-operation. As we have seen,

adolescents may test the boundaries, but if you respond with firmness and consistency, this will be a passing phase.

However, if you have taken on a rescued Border Terrier who has not been trained or socialised, or if you encounter problems with your dog as his training progresses, you will need to take action in order to avoid conflict and to stop the situation from worsening.

Many owners have reported that the Border Terrier is a 'people watcher' and, given the opportunity, he will attempt to control a situation. A Border Terrier will find something he values, and may then become possessive in order to guard what he sees as a valuable resource. This may take a number of different forms:

- A Border Terrier may become possessive over his food bowl, and growl if you approach him when he is eating.
- He may adopt a favourite toy

Teaching the retrieve is a good way of channelling chasing behaviour in a positive way.

Your dog may seek to guard something he values.

and refuse to give it up when requested.
- He may decide that the sofa is the best place to lie, and growl a warning if you ask him to move.

In each of these scenarios, the Border Terrier is determined to hang on to prized possession. Remember, a growl is a warning, and you do not want to do anything that will exacerbate his behaviour. For this reason, your aim is to avoid confrontation and allow him the opportunity to make a better choice:
- If your Border Terrier has taken up residence on the sofa,

distract his attention by showing him a toy or a treat and let him make the decision to jump off the sofa to get his reward.
- If he becomes possessive over toys, make sure you do not leave toys lying around. He only has the chance to play when you are interacting with him. When it is time to end the game, swap the toy with a treat.
- If he is guarding his food bowl, scatter some food around the bowl – and then into the bowl – when he is eating. In this way, he will welcome your presence rather than seeing it

as a threat.
- If he growls if you get too close to him when he is in his bed, make sure he is being given enough down time so he can rest undisturbed. Never force him to leave his bed, but encourage him by throwing treats at a distance so he has to get out of bed.
- If he becomes possessive over one person in the family, change the routine so he not always fed, cuddled, or exercised by 'his person'. Do not allow situations which encourage his guarding behaviour, and ensure that other members of the family

always offer a rewarding option so he chooses to interact with them.

You should also think about getting involved with a dog sport, such as agility or working trials, which will give your Border Terrier a positive outlet for his mental energy, and will also enhance your relationship with him.

However, if continues to show guarding behaviour, or you have any other concerns, do not delay in seeking professional help.

If you see signs of your Border Terrier becoming manipulative, you must work at lowering his status so that he realises that you are the leader and he does not have the right to guard resources. Although you need to be firm, you also need to use positive training methods so that your Border Terrier is rewarded for the behaviour you want. In this way, his 'correct' behaviour will be strengthened and repeated.

There are a number of steps you can take to teach your Border Terrier that you are in control. They include:

- Go back to basics and hold daily training sessions. Make sure you have some really tasty treats, or find a toy your Border Terrier really values and only bring it out at training sessions. Run through all the training exercises, and make a big fuss of your Border Terrier and reward him when he does well. This will reinforce the message that it is always rewarding to do as you ask.
- Teach your Border Terrier something new; this can be as simple as learning a trick, such as shaking paws. Having something new to think about will mentally stimulate your Border Terrier, and he will benefit from interacting with you.
- Be 100 per cent consistent with all house rules – your Border Terrier must never sit on the sofa (reward him for lying on his bed or on the floor) and you must never allow him to jump up at you (reward him for sitting when he greets you). This will make him more likely to repeat the desired behaviour.
- If your Border Terrier has been guarding his food bowl, put the bowl down empty, and drop in a little food at a time. Periodically stop dropping in the food, and tell your Border Terrier to "Sit" and "Wait". Give it a few seconds, and then reward him by dropping in more food. He will quickly learn that having you around at mealtimes is a good thing. Make sure the family eats before you feed your Border

Terrier. Some trainers advocate eating in front of the dog (maybe just a few bites from a biscuit) before starting a training session, so the dog appreciates your elevated status.

Teach your dog a new trick so you can reward 'good' behaviour.

- Do not let your Border Terrier barge through doors ahead of you or leap from the back of the car before you release him. You may need to put your dog on the lead and teach him to "Wait" at doorways, and then reward him for letting you go through first.

If your Border Terrier is progressing well with his retraining programme, think about getting involved with a dog sport, such as agility or working trials. This will give your Border Terrier a positive outlet for his energies. However, if your Border Terrier is still resource guarding, or you have any other concerns, do not delay in seeking the help of an animal behaviourist.

SEPARATION ANXIETY

The Border Terrier thrives on human companionship, but if he is brought up to accept short periods of separation from his owner, there is no reason why he should become anxious. A new puppy should be left for short periods on his own, ideally in a crate where he cannot get up to any mischief. It is a good idea to leave him with a boredom-busting toy (see page 58) so he will be happily occupied in your absence. When you return, do not rush to the crate and make a huge fuss. Wait a few minutes, and then calmly go to the crate and release your dog, telling him how good he has been. If this scenario is repeated a number of times, your Border Terrier will soon learn that being left on his own is no big deal.

AGGRESSION

Aggression is a complex issue, as there are different causes and the behaviour may be triggered by numerous factors. It may be directed towards people, but far

A well-bred Border Terrier that has been socialised will not have a trace of aggression in his make-up.

more commonly it is directed towards other dogs. Aggression in dogs may be the result of:

- Dog to dog animosity.
- Assertive behaviour: If behaviour, such as resource guarding (see page 111) is allowed to escalate..
- Defensive behaviour: This may be induced by fear, pain or punishment.
- Territory: A dog may become aggressive if strange dogs or people enter his territory (which is generally seen as the house and garden).
- Intra-sexual issues: This is aggression between sexes – male-to-male or female-to-female.
- Parental instinct: A mother dog may become aggressive if she is protecting her puppies.

A dog who has been well socialised (see page 104) and has been given sufficient exposure to other dogs at significant stages of his development will rarely be aggressive. A well-bred Border Terrier that has been reared correctly should not have a hint of aggression in his temperament. Obviously, if you have taken on an older, rescued dog, you will have little or no knowledge of his background, and if he shows signs of aggression, the cause will need to be determined. In most cases, you should call in professional help if you see aggressive behaviour in your dog; if the aggression is directed towards people, you should seek immediate advice. This behaviour can escalate very quickly and could lead to disastrous consequences.

NEW CHALLENGES

If you enjoy training your Border Terrier, you may want to try one of the many dog sports that are now on offer.

GOOD CITIZEN SCHEME

This is a scheme run by the Kennel Club in the UK and the American Kennel Club in the USA. The schemes promote responsible ownership and help you to train a well-behaved dog who will fit in with the community. The schemes are excellent for all pet owners, and they are also a good starting point if you plan to compete with your Border Terrier when he is older. The KC and the AKC schemes vary in format. In the UK there is puppy foundation, and then three levels: bronze, silver and gold, with each test becoming progressively more demanding. In the AKC scheme there is a single test.

Some of the exercises include:

- Walking on a loose lead among people and other dogs.
- Recall amid distractions.
- A controlled greeting where dogs stay under control while owners meet.
- The dog allows all-over grooming and handling by his owner, and will also accept being handled by the examiner.
- Stays, with the owner in sight, and then out of sight.
- Food manners, allowing the owner to eat without begging, and taking a treat on command.
- Sendaway – sending the dog to his bed.

The tests are designed to show the control you have over your dog, and his ability to respond correctly and remain calm in all situations. The Good Citizen Scheme is taught at most training clubs. For more information, log on to the Kennel Club or AKC website.

SHOWING

In your eyes, your Border Terrier is the most beautiful dog in the world – but would a judge agree? Showing is a highly competitive sport and often involves long days away from home. However, many owners get bitten by the showing bug, and their calendar is governed by the dates of the top showing fixtures.

To be successful in the show ring, a Border Terrier must conform as closely as possible to the Breed Standard, which is a written blueprint describing the 'perfect' Border Terrier (see Chapter Seven). To get started you need to buy a puppy that has show potential and then train him to perform in the ring. A Border Terrier will be expected to stand in show pose, gait for the judge in order to show off his natural movement, and to be examined by the judge. This involves a detailed hands-on examination, so your Border Terrier must be bombproof when handled by strangers.

Many training clubs hold

Showing is highly competitive at the top level.

ringcraft classes, which are run by experienced showgoers. At these classes, you will learn how to handle your Border Terrier in the ring, and you will also find out about rules, procedures and show ring etiquette. The best plan is to start off at some small, informal shows where you can practise and learn the tricks of the trade before graduating to bigger shows. It's a long haul starting in the very first puppy class, but the dream is to make your Border Terrier up into a Champion.

COMPETITIVE OBEDIENCE

Border Collies and German Shepherds dominate this sport, and in the UK it is rare for the terrier breeds to compete at the highest level. However, there is no doubt that the Border Terrier has the intelligence required, if you are prepared to put in the hard work. The classes start off being relatively easy and become progressively more challenging with additional exercises and the handler giving minimal instructions to the dog.

Exercises include:

- **Heelwork:** Dog and handler must complete a set pattern on and off the lead, which includes left turns, right turns, about turns, and changes of pace.
- **Recall:** This may be when the handler is stationary or on the move.
- **Retrieve:** This may be a dumbbell or any article chosen by the judge.
- **Sendaway:** The dog is sent to a designated spot and must go into an instant Down until he is recalled by the handler.

- **Stays:** The dog must stay in the Sit and in the Down for a set amount of time. In advanced classes, the handler is out of sight.
- **Scent:** The dog must retrieve a single cloth from a pre-arranged pattern of cloths that has his owner's scent, or, in advanced classes, the judge's scent. There may also be decoy cloths.
- **Distance control.** The dog must execute a series of moves (Sit, Stand, Down) without moving from his position and with the handler at a distance.

Even though competitive obedience requires accuracy and precision, make sure you make it fun for your Border Terrier, with lots of praise and rewards so that you motivate him to do his best.

Border Terriers enjoy the challenge of agility, and a number have proved to be highly successful.

Many training clubs run advanced classes for those who want to compete in obedience, or you can hire the services of a professional trainer for one-on-one sessions.

RALLY

If you feel that the rigours of competitive obedience are too much for you and your Border Terrier, you may prefer a more relaxed sport which is known as Rally. This is loosely based on obedience, and also has a few exercises based on agility. Handler and dog must complete a course, in the designated order, which has a variety of different exercises that could number from 12 to 20. The course is timed and the team must complete within the time limit that is set, but there are no bonus marks for speed. As you and your dog gain experience, you can work your way up from level one to six.

AGILITY

This fun sport has grown enormously in popularity over the past few years, and the clever, speedy Border Terrier has certainly made his mark. If you fancy having a go, make sure you have good control over your Border Terrier so that his attention is focused on you, rather than going off in pursuit of an interesting scent. In agility competitions, each dog must complete a set course over a series of obstacles,

WORKING TRIALS

This is a very challenging sport, which has been adapted so that smaller breeds can also take part. The Border Terrier, with his excellent sense of smell, can be very successful. The sport consists of three basic components:

- **Control:** Dog and handler must complete obedience exercises, but the work does not have to be as precise as it is in competitive obedience.
- **Agility:** In Companion Dog (CD) and Utility Dog (UD) the jumps for dogs under 15 inches (38 cm), which should include all Border Terriers, are a 2 ft (0.60 m) hurdle, a 6 ft (1.82 m) long jump, and a 4 ft (1.22 m) scale.

- **Nosework:** The dog must follow a track that has been laid over a set course. The surface may vary, and the length of time between the track being laid and the dog starting work is increased in the advanced classes.

The ladder of stakes are: Companion Dog, Utility Dog, Working Dog, Tracking Dog and Patrol Dog. However, the heights of jumps are not reduced after Utility Dog stakes so Border Terriers cannot compete in the higher stakes. In the US, tracking is a sport in its own right, and is very popular among Border Terrier owners.

If you want to get involved in working trials, you will need to find a specialist club or a trainer that specialises in the sport.

which include:
- Jumps (upright hurdles and long jump)
- Weaves
- A-frame
- Dog walk
- Seesaw
- Tunnels
- Tyre

Dogs may compete in jumping classes with jumps, tunnels and weaves, or in agility classes, which have the full set of equipment. Faults are awarded for poles down on the jumps, missed contact points on the A-frame, dog walk and seesaw, and refusals. If a dog takes the wrong course, he is eliminated. The winner is the dog that completes the course in the fastest time with no faults. As you progress up the levels, courses become progressively harder with more twists, turns and changes of direction.

If you want to get involved in agility, you will need to find a club that specialises in the sport (see Appendices). You will not be allowed to start training until your Border Terrier is 12 months old, and you cannot compete until he is 18 months old. This rule is for the protection of the dog, who may suffer injury if he puts strain on bones and joints while he is still growing.

FLYBALL
Flyball is a team sport; the dogs love it, and it is undoubtedly the noisiest of all the canine sports! The Border Terrier takes part with gusto!

Four dogs are selected to run in a relay race against an opposing team. The dogs are sent out by their handlers to jump four hurdles, catch the ball from the flyball box, and then return over the hurdles.

At the top level, this sport is fast and furious, and although it is dominated by Border Collies, the Border Terrier can make a big contribution. This is particularly true in multibreed competitions where the team is

Spend time training and interacting with your Border Terrier, and you will be rewarded a hundredfold.

made up of four dogs of different breeds, and only one can be a Border Collie or a Working Sheepdog. Points are awarded to dogs and teams. Annual awards are given to top dogs and top teams, and milestone awards are given out to dogs as they attain points throughout their flyballing careers.

DANCING WITH DOGS

This sport is relatively new, but it is becoming increasingly popular. It is very entertaining to watch, but it is certainly not as simple as it looks. To perform a choreographed routine to music with your Border Terrier demands a huge amount of training.

Dancing with dogs is divided into two categories: heelwork to music and canine freestyle. In heelwork to music, the dog must work closely with his handler and show a variety of close 'heelwork' positions. In canine freestyle, the routine can be more flamboyant, with the dog working at a distance from the handler and performing spectacular tricks. Routines are judged on style and presentation, content and accuracy.

SUMMING UP

The Border Terrier is a wonderful companion dog – but he is not right for everyone. This is a dog who must have exercise and mental stimulation, so make sure you keep your half of the bargain: spend time socialising and training your Border Terrier so that you can be proud to take him anywhere and he will always be a credit to you.

THE PERFECT BORDER TERRIER

Chapter 7

In the dictionary, the word 'perfect' is defined as: "complete with all the necessary qualities, faultless and not deficient". If you were to ask anyone in the dog show world about what they would class as the perfect Border Terrier, they would answer that there is no such thing, as every dog has a fault. However, if you were to ask the same question to anyone who owns a pet Border Terrier, they would say they owned him! A pet owner is not looking for perfection as in the Breed Standard, but for the perfect companion. The Border Terrier has a super temperament, is affectionate and easy to live with, and is generally obedient – and so he comes pretty close to perfection as a pet dog.

The Breed Standard is the blueprint for the breed – and it describes the ideal Border Terrier in words. However, this can be interpreted in many ways, hence the variations of show results. One judge may put emphasis on certain points, while another judge may put emphasis on others. There is a further complication in that the Breed Standard varies slightly depending on the country where the Border Terrier is being judged.

There are three major governing bodies that oversee the world of pedigree dogs: the Kennel Club, which is the ruling body in the UK, the American Kennel Club in the USA, and the Fédération Cynologique Internationale (International Canine Federation – referred to as the FCI), which is an umbrella society for most of the European countries and some South American countries.

BECOMING A CHAMPION

At Championship shows in the UK, Challenge Certificates are awarded to the Best Dog and Best Bitch of each breed. To achieve the title of Champion, a dog must win three Challenge Certificates from three different Kennel Club approved judges. There is no time-scale involved – you could make up a Champion in just a few weeks or over several years.

In the USA, dogs compete in conformation shows for points towards their AKC Championships. A total of 15 points are needed, which must include two majors (wins of three, four and five points at one show) awarded by at least three different judges, to become an American Kennel Club 'Champion of Record'. The number of Championship points awarded depends on the number of males (dogs) and females (bitches) of the breed actually in competition. The larger the entry, the greater the number of points that a male or female can win.

It is a huge achievement to make up a Champion in the UK.

The maximum number of points awarded to a dog at any show is five points.

The FCI is the ruling body for International Shows, and the Certificate of Aptitude of International Champion of Beauty (otherwise know as CACIB) is awarded to recognised breeds at these shows. A dog has to win four CACIBs from three different national countries, at International Shows to gain its title of International Champion.

It has been long acknowledged that the most prestigious and difficult title to achieve is that of Champion in the UK. In most other countries once a dog achieves his Champion title he then has to move into the Champion class. This leaves the way open for other dogs to compete for their title without having to be judged alongside Champions. This makes it an easier title to achieve, as the best dogs are removed from the basic competition. The only time a dog who was competing for his title would meet a Champion is when the Best of Breed is judged and awarded. Obviously, I should add, with numerically large breeds,

even in overseas countries, it is not always easy to achieve the Champion title.

INTERPRETING THE BREED STANDARD

For me, the Breed Standard approved by the Kennel Club of the country of origin should be the one used by other kennel clubs worldwide, but perhaps because the Breed Standard for the Border Terrier is too simply written, other kennel clubs or other canine organisations have written their own for the breed, adding more description to it.

The FCI has a Breed Standard that is very similar to the KC version, but the American Kennel Club Standard is far more descriptive, and there are some significant differences in what is asked for. I will now look at both the KC and the AKC Standards and give my personal interpretation.

In 2009, following concern about the health of some dog breeds, the Kennel Club in the UK updated all Breed Standards to include the following introductory paragraph:

"A Breed Standard is the guideline which describes the ideal characteristics, temperament and appearance of a breed and ensures that the breed is fit for function. Absolute soundness is essential. Breeders and judges should at all times be careful to avoid obvious conditions or exaggerations which would be detrimental in any way to the health, welfare or soundness of this breed. From time to time certain conditions or exaggerations

This is an active, working terrier, who is strongly put together, and gives an impression of endurance and agility.

may be considered to have the potential to affect dogs in some breeds adversely, and judges and breeders are requested to refer to the Kennel Club website for details of any such current issues. If a feature or quality is desirable it should only be present in the right measure."

In the case of the Border Terrier – a sound, active breed without exaggeration – no other changes were made to the existing Breed Standard.

GENERAL APPEARANCE

KC
Essentially a working terrier.

AKC
He is an active terrier of medium bone, strongly put together, suggesting endurance and agility, but rather narrow in shoulder, body and quarter. The body is covered with a somewhat broken through close-fitting and intensely wiry jacket. The characteristic 'otter' head with its keen eye, combined with a body poise which is 'at the alert', gives a look of fearless and implacable determination characteristic of the breed. Since the Border Terrier is a working terrier of a size to go to ground, and able, within reason, to follow a horse, his conformation should be such that he be ideally built to do his job. No deviation from this ideal conformation should be permitted, which would impair his usefulness in running his quarry to earth and in bolting it there from. For his work he must be alert, active and agile, and capable of squeezing through narrow apertures and rapidly traversing any kind of terrain. His head 'like that of an otter' is distinctive, and his temperament ideally exemplifies that of a terrier. By nature he is good tempered, affectionate, obedient and easily trained. In the field he is as hard as nails 'game as they come' and driving in attack. It should be the aim of Border Terrier breeders to avoid such over emphasis of any point in the standard as might lead to unbalanced exaggeration.

The Border Terrier has been closely guarded by dedicated breeders ever since being recognised by the Kennel Club in 1920 with the aim of keeping the Border Terrier exactly as the first line of the Breed Standard states. First and foremost, he should look like a working terrier, capable of doing what he was bred for, without being sculptured and groomed into purely a show dog.

The Border Terrier is an easy-going dog who is happy to live alongside, and co-operate with, other dogs.

The very lengthy AKC description of general appearance gives the impression that the dog is required to be very alert at all times and is up for anything. This leads you to believe that this is how the dog should be in general everyday life. In fact, the Border Terrier is not like this, nor was it the intention of those who developed the breed.

CHARACTERISTICS AND TEMPERAMENT

KC
Characteristics: Capable of following a horse, combining activity with gameness. Temperament: Active and game as previously stated.

AKC
His temperament ideally exemplifies that of a terrier. By nature he is good tempered, affectionate, obedient and easily trained. In the field he is hard as nails, 'game as they come' and driving in attack.

The Border Terrier was originally bred to follow a horse (as Foxhounds do) but that would not mean a Thoroughbred. The terrain of the Border Foxhounds, which is where the Border Terrier gets its name, would require a slower and more substantial type of hunter. The requirement of "combining activity with gameness" calls for a lively, spirited dog with sound movement.

I would like to add to the description of temperament that a Border Terrier should be easygoing, amenable and friendly with both humans and other dogs. He should be sound in mind – not too excitable, not hot-headed – but showing a kind and affectionate disposition, and being calm in everyday situations. He should be agreeable when working with other terriers.

HEAD AND SKULL

KC
Head like that of an otter, moderately broad in skull, with a short strong muzzle. Black nose preferable, but a liver or flesh coloured one not a serious fault.

The 'otter' head is a unique feature of the Border Terrier and makes him stand out from all the other terrier breeds.

It is helpful to study photos of otters in order to understand the breed requirement for a Border Terrier's head.

AKC

Similar to that of an otter. Moderately broad and flat in skull with plenty of width between the eyes and between the ears. A slightly moderate broad curve at the stop rather than a pronounced indentation. Cheeks slightly full. Muzzle short and 'well filled'. A dark muzzle is characteristic and desirable. A few short whiskers are natural to the breed. Nose black, of good size.

This part of the Breed Standard is perhaps one of the most important statements that differentiates the Border Terrier from all the other terrier breeds. If a Border Terrier does not possess the classic otter head, the dog will lack type, and could be just another terrier. The otter-like head is the one thing that symbolises the breed. If you are unsure of this distinct head shape, then study and research otters, and it will soon become apparent. The nose colour being

black certainly gives a more pleasing picture.

EYES

KC

Dark with keen expression.

AKC

Eyes dark hazel and full of fire and intelligence. Moderate in size, neither prominent nor small and beady.

The eyes should be dark and

The dark eyes should have a keen expression, but there should also be an element of softness, giving a kindly look.

should be slightly oval. They should not be prominent or round, not too close together and not too wide apart. When eye shape and eye set are incorrect, it can completely change the expression of the dog. When the muzzle is too short, this can often go along with round, prominent eyes, which will give a strange expression. Eyes should be keen, but not have a hard expression. Border Terrier eyes should still have a soft, kind eye, but these can still be keen.

The AKC description "full of fire and intelligence" instead of "dark with keen expression", would lead me to think that the dog had a menacing eye, although the Border has a kind eye.

EARS

KC
Small V-shaped of moderate thickness, dropping close to the cheek.

AKC
Ears V-shaped and of moderate thickness, dark preferred. Not set high on the head but somewhat on the side, and dropping forward close to the cheeks. They should not break above the level of the skull.

The ears should not be round, heavy or thick-skinned to the feel, but should be small and V-shaped, lying close to the cheek. They should not be set high on the skull, making them look close together, which would give a Fox Terrier expression. Neither should they break the top line of the skull. Ears should not hang or stick out away from the head or 'fly' as sometimes described.

MOUTH

KC
Scissor bite, i.e. the upper teeth closely overlapping the lower teeth, and set square to the jaw. A level bite acceptable. Undershot or overshot a major fault and highly undesirable.

AKC
Teeth strong with a scissor bite, large in proportion to the size of dog.

Scissor bite describes the dentition exactly. In an undershot bite, the front teeth (incisors) of the lower jaw project beyond the front teeth of the upper jaw when the mouth is closed. This is the type of dentition seen on a Bulldog, for example. In an overshot bite, the front teeth (incisors) of the upper jaw overlap and do not touch the front teeth of the lower jaw, leaving a big gap when the

The teeth should meet in a scissor bite, with the upper teeth closely overlapping the lower teeth.

FOREQUARTERS

KC
Forelegs straight and not too heavy in bone.

AKC
Shoulders well laid back and of good length, the blades converging to the withers gradually from a brisket not excessively deep or narrow. Forelegs straight and not too heavy in bone and placed slightly wider than in a Fox Terrier.

The forelegs should be straight when viewed from the front, neither wide apart nor turning in or out when viewed from the front. We do not want heavy, round, coarse bone or fine, light and weak bone. The bone should be moderate, clean and flat, giving a certain quality to the Border Terrier. When viewed from the side, the pasterns should be short, strong and have a slight slope. At the top of the leg, the upper arm slopes to meet the shoulderblade, which should be clean and sloping well back.

BODY

KC
Deep, narrow, fairly long. Ribs carried well back, but not over sprung, as a terrier should be

capable of being spanned by both hands behind the shoulder. Loin strong.

AKC
Back strong but laterally supple, with no suspicion of dip behind the shoulder. Loin strong. Body deep, fairly narrow and of sufficient length to avoid any suggestions of lack of range and agility.

mouth is closed. It can also be called pig-jawed or pig-mouthed, as pigs have this type of jaw.

NECK

KC
Of moderate length.

AKC
Neck clean, muscular and only long enough to give a well balanced appearance. It should gradually widen into the shoulder.

The Border Terrier's neck should not be short and stubby as if he has no neck and the head fits straight on to the shoulders. Neither should it be too long, giving a swan-like appearance. The neck should be well set on, merging gradually to the withers, forming a pleasing transition into the topline/backline. The neck should not have an upper arched portion of the neck – for example, a crest.

The forelegs should be straight, with moderate bone which gives a sense of quality.

The body is narrow and fairly long and should be rectangular rather than square. Note the 'carrot-shaped' tail.

The body should be capable of being spanned by a man's hand behind the shoulders. Brisket not excessively deep or narrow. Deep ribs being carried well back and not over sprung in view of the desired depth and narrowness of the body. The underline fairly straight.

The body should be deep, but not too deep. The ribcage (sternum) is lower than the point of the elbow joint. It should be narrow and fairly long, giving the impression of the dog being slightly rectangular in body; he should never appear square. The ribs are carried well back but not over sprung. The ribcage is long, being approximately two-thirds of the body, with a moderate spring of rib. The ribcage should not be short, as this gives the rib a barrel-shaped appearance. Also, the ribs should never be flat or slab-sided. The underline is gradual – not the tucked-up appearance of the Whippet underline.

The body should be spannable; it should not be too large or the dog will not be able to go to ground to get to the quarry. The loin, which is on the top of the dog and lies between the finish of the ribs to the hindquarters, should be strong and short.

HINDQUARTERS

KC
Racy.

AKC
Muscular and racy, with thighs long and nicely moulded. Stifles well bent and hocks well let down.

The hindquarters should give the impression of speed without loss of substance. They should be long from hip to hock, short from hock to foot, with a good bend of stifle and without exaggeration. This means that the hind leg should neither be straight nor over angulated.

The 'racy' hindquarters should give an impression of speed.

as opposed to thick-soled shoes – it is much more comfortable to walk on stony and uneven ground wearing the thick-soled shoes, so we can compare the Border Terrier as having thick soles on his feet.

TAIL

KC
Moderately short, fairly thick at the base, then tapering. Set high, carried gaily, but not carried over the back.

AKC
Tail moderately short, thick at the base then tapering. Not set on too high. Carried gaily when at the alert, but not over the back. When at ease a Border Terrier may drop his stern.

The tail is best described as carrot-like in shape; it should never be carried in a sabre shape. It is set high, but not as high as a Fox Terrier, for example, which has a very high tail-set coming off the end of the topline. The tail should be straight and not have any deformities, bends or 'kinks'. The tail is never docked.

GAIT

KC
Has the soundness to follow a horse.

AKC
Straight and rhythmical before and behind, with good length of stride and flexing of the stifle and hock. The dog should respond to his handler with a gait which is free, agile and quick.

The Border Terrier should be long striding, free at all paces with

FEET

KC
Small with thick pads.

AKC
Feet small and compact. Toes should point forward and be moderately arched with thick pads.

Small, tight feet are called for; the toes should not be open, spread or flat in shape. Thick pads give a cushioning effect and extra protection to the foot to stand up to a day's work on the rough terrain that the dog would possibly have to go over. This can be likened to wearing thin-soled shoes

GAIT AND MOVEMENT

The front action is straight and should reach well forward.

The hind legs provide the drive.

A working terrier needs a harsh weather-resistant coat to protect him from the worst conditions.

good drive. The front action should be straight and reach well forward. The hocks should not turn in or out. Good movement is essential to allow the dog to follow a horse on a day's hunting.

COAT

KC
Harsh and dense, with close undercoat. Skin must be thick.

AKC
A short and dense undercoat covered with a very wiry and somewhat broken topcoat which should lie closely, but must not show any tendency to curl or wave. With such a coat a Border should be able to be exhibited almost in his natural state, nothing more in the way of trimming being needed than a tidying of the head, neck and feet. Hide very thick and loose fitting.

A stiff, wire coat is required. It should be dense with a short, soft undercoat to give the dog protection against the elements while working. The topcoat should never be soft or long. The skin or pelt should be thick to give protection from the quarry, and loose to enable the dog to manoeuvre himself in tight situations underground.

COLOUR

KC
Red, wheaten, grizzle and tan or blue and tan.

AKC
Red, grizzle and tan, blue and tan or wheaten. A small amount of white may be allowed on the chest but white on the feet should be penalized. A dark muzzle is characteristic and desirable.

The true wheaten is unseen in the present day and is often mistaken for light red. A true red has become rare, but can be found in certain kennels and bloodlines. Most Border Terriers are grizzle and tan, varying from pale tan to a very deep red tan. Blue and tan, which was rare in the past, has now become more popular and many Border Terriers of this colour can now be seen.

SIZE

KC

Dogs 5.9 kg to 7.1 kg (13 lbs to 15.5 lbs) Bitches 5.1 kg to 6.4 kg (11.5 lbs to 14 lbs).

AKC

Weight: Dogs, 13-15.5 pounds, bitches, 11.5-14 pounds, are appropriate weights for Border Terriers in hardworking condition. The proportions should be that height to the withers is slightly greater than the distance from the withers to the tail, i.e. by possibly 1-1.5 inches in a 14-pound dog. Of medium bone, strongly put together, suggesting endurance and agility, but rather narrow in shoulder, body and quarter.

Today, it is not uncommon to see Border Terriers much above the size stipulated in the KC Breed Standard. The AKC

SCALE OF POINTS

AKC

Head, ears, neck and teeth	20
Legs and feet	15
Coat and skin	10
Shoulders and chest	10
Eyes and expression	10
Back and loin	10
Hindquarters	10
Tail	5
General appearance	10
Total	100

Standard gives a real guide to the shape of the dog. This description actually gives you the idea of a squarer dog, i.e. shorter in back, whereas the UK Standard only states "fairly long", leaving it to the individual judge to assess the overall balance of the dog.

FAULTS

KC

Any departure from the foregoing points should be considered a fault and the seriousness with which the fault should be regarded should be in exact proportion to its degree and its effect on the terrier's ability to work, and

the health and welfare of the dog.
Note: Male animals should have two apparently normal testicles fully descended into the scrotum.

SUMMING UP

Comparing the two Breed Standards, I would say that the American version gives the impression that the Border Terrier is required to be alert, almost feisty, most of the time. The shape of the dog preferred in the USA would also be slightly different from that which is described in the KC Breed Standard.

Personally, I would prefer a less descriptive Breed Standard than the American version, avoiding much of the duplication that is evident throughout. As Anne Roslin-Williams, an English author and breeder of Border Terriers, wrote in her book *The Border Terrier* when discussing the KC Standard: *"Although the Standard has been criticised for leaving too much to the imagination, I maintain that if one knows the job of a working terrier, and has taken the trouble to find out from a good source, the basic anatomy of a dog, the Standard puts the finishing stitches to the tapestry of the Border."*

HAPPY AND HEALTHY

Chapter 8

The Border Terrier is a stoical dog with a life-span that runs into double figures, provided his needs are met. Although he has many of the terrier traits, the Border Terrier is renowned as a plucky, faithful companion and a willing, unconditional friend. He will, however, out of necessity, rely on you for food and shelter, accident prevention and medication. A healthy Border Terrier is a happy chap, looking to please and amuse his owner.

There are very few genetic conditions recognised in the Border Terrier. These will be covered in depth later in the chapter.

ROUTINE HEALTH CARE

VACCINATION

There is currently much debate over the issue of vaccination. The timing of the final part of the initial vaccination course for a puppy and the frequency of subsequent booster vaccinations are both under scrutiny. An evaluation of the relative risk for each disease plays a part, depending on the local situation. Many owners think that the actual vaccination is the protection, so that their puppy can go out for walks as soon as he has had the final part of the puppy vaccination course. This is not the case. The rationale behind vaccination is to stimulate the immune system into producing protective antibodies, which will be triggered if the patient is subsequently exposed to that particular disease. This means that a further one or two weeks will have to pass before an effective level of protection will have developed.

Vaccines against viruses stimulate longer-lasting protection than those against bacteria, whose effect may only persist for a matter of months in some cases. There is also the possibility of a dog's immune system not fully responding to a vaccination; although the vaccine schedule may have been followed as recommended, that particular dog will remain vulnerable. An individual dog's level of protection against rabies, as demonstrated by the antibody titre in a blood sample, is routinely tested in the UK in order to fulfil the requirements of the Pet Travel Scheme (PETS). This is not the case with other diseases, where there is not a system in place to gauge the need for booster vaccination or to determine the effect of a course of vaccines. Instead, your veterinary surgeon will advise a protocol based upon the vaccines available, local disease prevalence, and the lifestyle of you and your dog.

It is worth remembering that maintaining a fully effective level of immune protection against the disease, appropriate to your locale, is vital; these are serious diseases, which may be fatal to your dog, and some may have the potential to be passed on to humans (so-called zoonotic potential for transmission). This is where you will be grateful for your veterinary surgeon's knowledge and advice.

The American Animal Hospital Association laid down guidelines at the end of 2006 for the vaccination of dogs in North America. Core diseases were defined as distemper, adenovirus, parvovirus and rabies. So-called non-core diseases were listed as kennel cough, Lyme disease and leptospirosis; a decision to vaccinate against one or more non-core diseases is based on each dog's level of risk, determined on lifestyle and locality in the US.

Remember that the booster visit to the veterinary surgery is not 'just' for a booster. Instead, this appointment is a chance for a full health check and evaluation of how your dog is doing. After all, we are all familiar with the adage that one human year is

The vet will give your dog a thorough check-up when it is time for his booster injection.

equivalent to seven canine years. There have been attempts in recent times to re-set the scale for two reasons: small breeds live longer than giant breeds, and dogs are living longer than previously. I have seen dogs of 17 and 18 years of age, but to say a dog is 119 or 126 years old is plainly meaningless. It does, however, emphasise the fact that a dog's health can change dramatically over the course of a single year, because dogs age at a far greater rate than humans.

For me, as a veterinary surgeon, the booster vaccination visit is a challenge: how much can I find of which the owner was unaware, such as rotten teeth or a heart murmur? Even

monitoring bodyweight year upon year is of use, because bodyweight can creep up or down without an owner realising. Being overweight is unhealthy, but it may take an outsider's remark to make an owner realise that there is a problem. Conversely, a drop in bodyweight may be the only pointer to an underlying problem.

The diseases against which dogs are vaccinated include:

ADENOVIRUS
Canine Adenovirus 1 (CAV-1) affects the liver (hepatitis) and the classic 'blue eye' appearance in some affected dogs, whilst CAV-2 is a cause of kennel cough (see later). Vaccines often include both canine adenoviruses.

DISTEMPER
This is also called 'hardpad' due to the characteristic changes to the pads of the paws. It is a worldwide problem, but fortunately vaccination has been very effective at reducing its occurrence. It is caused by a virus and affects the respiratory, gastro-intestinal (gut) and nervous systems, so it causes a wide range of illnesses. Fox and urban stray dog populations are most at risk, and therefore responsible for local outbreaks.

KENNEL COUGH
This is also known as infectious tracheobronchitis. Bordetella bronchiseptica is not only a

major cause of kennel cough, but also a common secondary infection on top of another cause. Being a bacterium, it is susceptible to treatment with appropriate antibiotics, but the immunity stimulated by the vaccine is therefore short-lived (six to 12 months).

This vaccine is often in a form to be administered down the nostrils in order to stimulate local immunity at the point of entry. Do not be alarmed to see your veterinary surgeon using a needle and syringe to draw up the vaccine, because the needle will be replaced with a special plastic introducer, allowing the vaccine to be gently instilled into each nostril. Dogs generally resent being held more than the actual intra-nasal vaccine, and I have learnt that covering the patient's eyes helps greatly.

However, kennel cough is rather a catch-all term for any cough spreading within a dog population, not just in kennels but also between dogs at a training session or breed show, or even mixing out in the park. Many of these infections may not be B. bronchiseptica but other viruses, for which one can only treat symptomatically. Parainfluenza virus is often included in a vaccine programme because it is a common viral cause of kennel cough.

Kennel cough can seem alarming. There is a persistent cough accompanied by the production of white frothy spittle, which can last for a

Kennel cough spreads rapidly among dogs that live together.

matter of weeks, during which time the patient is highly infectious to other dogs. I remember when it ran through our five Border Collies – there were white patches of froth on the floor wherever you looked! Other features include sneezing, a runny nose, and eyes sore with conjunctivitis. Fortunately, these infections are generally self-limiting and most dogs recover without any long-lasting problems, but an elderly dog may be knocked sideways by it, akin to the effects of a common cold on a frail, elderly person.

LEPTOSPIROSIS

Contact with rats and their urine is the common way that dogs contract this disease, also known as Weil's disease in humans. This is a zoonotic disease with implications for all those in contact with an affected dog.

The UK National Rodent Survey 2003 found a wild brown rat population of 60 million, equivalent at the time to one rat per person. There is an equal risk for the Border Terrier living with a family on the edge of a town as the Border Terrier exploring ditches, ponds and farmland in the countryside.

The situation in the US is less clear-cut. Blanket vaccination against leptospirosis is not considered necessary because it only occurs in certain areas, so you must be guided by your veterinarian.

LYME DISEASE

This is a bacterial infection transmitted by hard ticks. It is therefore prevalent in specific areas of the US where ticks are found, such as north-eastern states, some southern states, California and the upper Mississippi region. It does also occur in the UK, but at a low

Lyme disease is transmitted by ticks and is more likely to affect dogs that live in rural areas.

level, so vaccination is not routinely offered.

Clinical disease is manifested primarily as limping due to arthritis, but other organs affected include the heart, kidneys and nervous system. It is readily treatable with appropriate antibiotics once diagnosed, but the causal bacterium, Borrelia burgdorferi, is not cleared from the body totally and will persist.

Prevention requires both vaccination and tick control, especially as there are other diseases transmitted by ticks. Ticks carrying B. burgdorferi will transmit it to humans as well, but an infected dog cannot pass it to a human.

PARVOVIRUS

This appeared in the late 1970s, when it was thought that the UK's dog population would be decimated by it. This was a notion that terrified me at the time but fortunately it did not happen on the scale envisaged. Occurrence is mainly low now, thanks to vaccination. It is also occasionally seen in the elderly, unvaccinated dog.

RABIES

This is another zoonotic disease and there are very strict control measures in place. Vaccines were once only available in the UK on an individual basis for dogs being taken abroad. Pets travelling into

the UK had to serve six months' compulsory quarantine so that any pet incubating rabies would be identified before being released back into the general population. Under the Pet Travel Scheme, provided certain criteria are met (refer to the DEFRA website for up-to-date information – www.defra.gov.uk) then dogs can re-enter the UK without being quarantined.

Dogs to be imported into the US have to show that they were vaccinated against rabies at least 30 days previously; otherwise, they have to serve effective internal quarantine for 30 days from the date of vaccination against rabies, in order to ensure they are not incubating the disease. The exception is dogs entering from countries recognised as being rabies-free, in which case it has to be proved that they lived in that country for at least six months beforehand.

PARASITES

A parasite is defined as an organism deriving benefit on a one-way basis from another; the host. It goes without saying that it is not to the parasite's advantage to harm the host to such an extent that the benefit is lost, especially if it results in the death of the host.

This means a dog could harbour parasites, internal and/or external, without there being any signs apparent to the owner. Many canine parasites can, however, transfer to humans with variable consequences, so routine preventative treatment is advised against particular parasites. Just as with vaccination, risk assessment plays a part; for example, there is no need for routine heartworm treatment in the UK (at present), but it is vital in the US and in Mediterranean countries.

INTERNAL PARASITES

ROUNDWORMS (NEMATODES)

These are the spaghetti-like worms that you may have been unfortunate enough to have seen passed in faeces or brought up in vomit. Most of the deworming treatments in use today cause the adult roundworms to disintegrate, thankfully, so that treating puppies in particular is not as unpleasant as it used to be! Most puppies will have a worm burden, mainly of a particular roundworm species (Toxocara canis), which reactivates within the mother's tissues during pregnancy and passes to the foetuses developing in the womb. It is therefore important to treat the dam both during and after pregnancy, as well as the puppies.

Professional advice is to continue worming every month. There are roundworm eggs in the environment, and unless you examine your dog's faeces under a microscope on a very regular basis for their presence, you will be unaware of your dog having picked up roundworms, unless he should have such a heavy burden that he passes the adults.

It takes a few weeks from the time that a dog swallows a Toxocara canis roundworm egg to the passing of viable eggs (the pre-patent period). There are deworming products that are active all the time, which will provide continuous protection when administered as often as directed. Otherwise, treating every month will, in effect, cut in before a dog could theoretically become a source of roundworm eggs to the general population.

It is the risk to human health that is so important: T. canis roundworms will migrate within our tissues and cause all manner of problems, not least of which is blindness. If a dog has roundworms, the eggs also find their way on to his coat where they can be picked up during stroking and cuddling. You should always carefully pick up your dog's faeces and dispose of them appropriately. This will not only reduce the chance for environmental contamination with all manner of infections, but will also make walking more pleasant underfoot.

TAPEWORMS (CESTODES)

When considering the general dog population, the primary source of the commonest tapeworm species will be fleas, which can carry the eggs. Most multi-wormers will be active against these tapeworms, not because they are a hazard to human health, but because it is unpleasant to see the wriggly rice-grain tapeworm segments emerging from your dog's back passage while he is lying in front of the fire, and usually when you have had guests for dinner.

All puppies should be routinely treated for roundworm.

There are specific requirements for treatment with praziquantel within 24 to 48 hours of return into the UK under the PETS. This is to prevent the inadvertent introduction of Echinococcus multilocularis, a tapeworm carried by foxes on mainland Europe; it is transmissible to humans, causing serious or even fatal liver disease.

HEARTWORM (DIROFILARIA IMMITIS)

Heartworm infection has been diagnosed in dogs all over the world. There are two prerequisites: the presence of mosquitoes and a warm, humid climate. When a female mosquito bites an infected animal, it acquires D. immitis in its circulating form, as microfilariae. A warm environmental temperature is needed for these microfilariae to develop into the infective third-stage larvae (L3) within the mosquitoes, the so-called intermediate host. L3 larvae are then transmitted by the mosquito when it next bites a dog. Therefore, while heartworm infection is found in all the states of the US, it is at such differing levels that an occurrence in Alaska, for example, is probably a reflection of a visiting dog having previously picked up the infection elsewhere.

Heartworm infection is not

In adult dogs, a worming programme is an essential part of preventative health care.

currently a problem in the UK, except for those dogs contracting it while abroad, without suitable preventative treatment. Global warming and its effect on the UK's climate, however, could change that. It is a potentially life-threatening condition, with dogs of all breeds and ages being susceptible without preventative treatment. The larvae can grow to 14 inches within the right side of the heart, causing primarily signs of heart failure and ultimately liver and kidney damage. It can be treated, but

prevention is a better plan. In the US, regular blood tests for the presence of infection are advised, coupled with appropriate preventative measures, so I would advise liaising with your veterinary surgeon.

For dogs travelling to heartworm-endemic areas of the EU, such as the Mediterranean coast, preventative treatment should be started before leaving the UK and maintained during the visit. Again, this is best arranged with your veterinary surgeon.

EXTERNAL PARASITES

FLEAS

There are several species of flea, which are not host-specific; not only can a dog be carrying cat and human fleas as well as dog fleas, but also the same flea treatment will kill and/or control them all. It is also accepted that environmental control is a vital part of a flea-control programme. This is because the adult flea is only on the animal for as long as it takes to have a blood meal and to breed; the remainder of the life cycle occurs in the house, car, caravan, shed etc…

There is a vast array of flea-control products available, with various routes of administration: collar, powder, spray, 'spot-on',

Cats are often responsible for the transmission of fleas.

oral. Flea control needs to be applied to all pets in the house, independent of whether they leave the house, as fleas can be introduced by other pets and their human owners. It is best to discuss your specific flea-control needs with your veterinary surgeon.

MITES

There are five types of mite that can affect dogs:

Demodex canis: This mite is a normal inhabitant of canine hair follicles, passed from the bitch to her pups as they suckle. The development of actual skin disease or demodicosis depends on the individual. Some Border Terriers may develop the generalised form of demodicosis for the first time in middle-age (more than four years of age).

Sarcoptes scabei: This characteristically causes an intense pruritus or itchiness in the affected dog, causing him to scratch incessantly and bite at himself, leading to marked fur loss and skin trauma. Initially starting on the elbows, earflaps and hocks, without treatment the skin on the rest of the body can become affected, with thickening and pigmentation of the skin.

Cheyletiella yasguri: This is the fur mite most commonly found on dogs. It is often called 'walking dandruff' because it can be possible to see collections of the small white mite moving about over the skin surface.

Otodectes cynotis: A highly transmissible otitis externa (outer ear infection) results from the presence in the outer ear canal of this ear mite, characterised by exuberant production of dark earwax. The patient will frequently shake his head and rub at the ear(s). The mites can also spread on to the skin adjacent to the opening of the external ear canal, and may transfer elsewhere, such as the paws.

(Neo-) Trombicula autumnalis: The free-living harvest mite can cause an intense local irritation on the skin. Its larvae are picked up from undergrowth, so they are characteristically found as a bright orange patch on the web of skin between the digits of the paws. It feeds on skin cells before dropping off to complete its life cycle in the environment.

Your veterinary surgeon will be able to diagnose and recommend suitable treatments for each of these types of mite.

TICKS

Ticks have become an increasing problem in recent years throughout Britain. Rough, long grass is a major habitat. Their physical presence causes irritation, but it is their potential to spread disease, such as Lyme disease, that causes concern.

ALABAMA ROT

This is a rare, but deadly disease that is now being reported in the UK. The first sign of disease, which damages blood vessels and the kidney, is red or inflamed skin that develops into ulcer-like sores. They are most frequently found below the knee or elbow, and occasionally on the stomach or face.

Early detection is essential but even so, there is only a 30 per cent chance that treatment will be successful.

It is thought that the disease may be spread from wooded and muddy areas, and so the advice is to wash mud from your dog as soon as you return from a walk, as well as restricting access to such areas.

Removing a tick is simple – provided your dog will stay still. The important rule is to twist gently so that the tick is persuaded to let go with its mouth-parts. Grasp the body of the tick as near to your dog's skin as possible, either between thumb and fingers or with a specific tick-removing instrument, and then rotate in one direction until the tick comes away.

There were said to be classic pockets of ticks in the UK, such as the New Forest and Thetford Forest, but they are actually found nationwide. The life cycle is curious; each life stage takes a year to develop and move on to the next.

Long grass is a major habitat. The vibration of animals moving through the grass will stimulate the larva, nymph or adult to climb up a blade of grass and wave its legs in the air as it 'quests' for a host on which to latch for its next blood meal. Humans are as likely to be hosts as dogs, so ramblers and orienteerers are advised to cover their legs when going through rough, long grass, tucking the ends of their trousers into their socks.

As well as their physical presence causing irritation, it is the potential for disease transmission that is of concern. A tick will transmit any infection previously contracted while feeding on an animal – for example Borrelia burgdorferi, the causal agent of Lyme disease (see 136).

A-Z OF COMMON AILMENTS

ANAL SACS, IMPACTED
The anal sacs lie on either side of the back passage or anus at approximately four and eight o'clock, if compared with the face of a clock. They fill with a particularly pungent fluid, which is emptied on to the faeces as they move past the sacs to exit from the anus. Theories abound as to why these sacs should become impacted periodically, and seemingly more so in some dogs than others. The irritation of impacted anal sacs is often seen as 'scooting', when the backside is dragged along the ground. Some dogs will gnaw at their back feet or over the rump.

Increasing the fibre content of the diet helps some dogs; in others, underlying skin disease is the cause. It may be a one-off occurrence for no apparent reason.

Sometimes, an infection can become established, requiring antibiotic therapy, which may need to be coupled with flushing out the infected sac under sedation or general anaesthesia. More rarely, a dog will present with an apparently acute-onset anal sac abscess, which is incredibly painful.

DIARRHOEA
Cause and treatment much as Gastritis (see below).

EAR INFECTIONS
The dog has a long external ear canal, initially vertical then horizontal, leading to the eardrum, which protects the middle ear. If your Border Terrier is shaking his head, then his ears will need to be inspected with an

auroscope by a veterinary surgeon in order to identify any cause and to ensure the eardrum is intact. A sample may be taken from the canal to be examined under the microscope and cultured to identify causal agents, before prescribing appropriate eardrops containing antibiotic, anti-fungal agent and/or steroid.

Predisposing causes of otitis externa or infection in the external ear canal include: presence of a foreign body such as a grass awn; ear mites, which are intensely irritating to the dog and stimulate the production of brown wax, predisposing to infection; previous infections causing the canal's lining to thicken, narrowing the canal and reducing ventilation; all swimming – some Border Terriers love swimming, but water trapped in the external ear canal can lead to infection, especially if the water is not clean.

FOREIGN BODIES (Internal)

Items swallowed in haste, without checking whether they can be digested, can cause problems if they lodge in the stomach or obstruct the intestines, necessitating surgical removal. Acute vomiting is the main indication. Common objects I have seen removed include stones from the garden, peach stones, babies' dummies, golf balls, and once a lady's bra!

It is possible to diagnose a dog with an intestinal obstruction across a waiting room from a particularly 'tucked-up' stance

Check your dog thoroughly if he has been exercising in long grass.

and pained facial expression. These patients bounce back from surgery dramatically. A previously docile and compliant obstructed patient will return for a post-operative check-up and literally bounce into the consulting room.

FOREIGN BODIES (External)

Grass awns are adept at finding their way into orifices such as a nostril, down an ear, and into the soft skin between two digits (toes), where they start a one-way journey, due to the direction of their whiskers. In particular, I remember a grass awn that migrated from a hind paw, causing abscesses along the way, but not yielding itself up until it erupted through the skin in the groin!

GASTRITIS

This is usually a simple stomach upset, most commonly in response to dietary indiscretion.

Scavenging constitutes a change in the diet as much as an abrupt switch in the food being fed by the owner. Generally, a day without food, followed by a few days of small, frequent meals of a bland diet (such as cooked chicken or fish or an appropriate prescription diet) should allow the stomach to settle. It is vital to wean the patient back on to routine food or else another bout of gastritis may occur.

JOINT PROBLEMS

It is not unusual for older Border Terriers to be stiff after exercise, particularly in cold weather. This is not really surprising, given that they are such busy dogs when young, rushing around in hedgerows and ditches. This is such a game breed that a nine- or ten-year-old Border Terrier will not readily forego an extra walk or take kindly to turning for home earlier than usual. Your veterinary surgeon will be able to advise you on ways to help your dog cope with stiffness, not least of which will be to ensure that he is not overweight. Arthritic joints do not need to be burdened with extra bodyweight!

LUMPS

Regularly handling and stroking your dog will help the early detection of lumps and bumps. These may be due to infection (abscess), bruising, multiplication of particular cells from within the body, or even an external parasite (tick). If you are worried about any lump you find, have it checked by a veterinary surgeon.

OBESITY

Being overweight does predispose to many other problems, such as diabetes mellitus, heart disease and joint problems. It is so easily prevented by simply acting as your Border Terrier's conscience. Ignore pleading eyes and feed according to your dog's waistline. The body condition is what matters qualitatively, alongside monitoring the dog's bodyweight as a quantitative measure. The Border Terrier should have at least a suggestion of a waist and it should be possible to feel the ribs beneath only a slight layer of fat.

Neutering does not automatically mean that your Border Terrier will be overweight. Having an ovario-hysterectomy does slow down the body's rate of working, castration to a lesser

Keep a close check on your Border Terrier's ears for any sign of infection.

extent, but it therefore means that your dog needs less food. I recommend cutting back a little on the amount of food fed a few weeks before neutering. If he looks a little underweight on the morning of the operation, it will help the veterinary surgeon as well as giving him a little leeway weight-wise afterwards. It is always harder to lose weight after neutering than before, because of this slowing in the body's inherent metabolic rate.

TEETH

Eating food starts with the dog gripping and killing his prey in the wild with the canine teeth; the incisor teeth bite off pieces of food and then the molars chew it. To be able to eat is vital for life, yet the actual health of the teeth is often overlooked; unhealthy teeth can predispose to disease, and not just by reducing the ability to eat. The presence of infection within the mouth can lead to bacteria entering the bloodstream and then filtering out at major organs, with the potential for serious consequences. Equally, simply having dental pain can affect a dog's well-being, as anyone who has had toothache will confirm. Veterinary dentistry has made huge leaps in recent years, so that it no longer consists of extraction as the treatment of necessity.

Good dental health lies in the hands of the owner, starting from the moment the dog comes into your care. Just as we have taken on responsibility for feeding, so we have acquired the task of maintaining good dental and oral hygiene. In an ideal world, we should brush our dogs' teeth as regularly as our own. The Border Terrier puppy who finds having his teeth brushed is a huge game and excuse to roll over and over on the ground requires loads of patience, twice a day.

There are alternative strategies, ranging from dental chewsticks to specially formulated foods, but the main thing is to be aware of your

The Border Terrier is a hardy breed with few inherited disorders.

dog's mouth. At least train your puppy to permit full examination of his teeth, which will not only ensure you are checking in his mouth regularly but will also make your veterinary surgeon's job easier when there is a real need for your dog to 'Open wide!'

BREED SPECIFIC HEALTH ISSUES

We are fortunate that the Border Terrier suffers from a very limited number of inherited or breed specific health issues. However, it is important that breeders are aware of possible problems and safeguard their breeding programmes to ensure the future health and wellbeing of the Border Terrier.

CANINE EPILEPTOID CRAMPING SYNDROME (CECS)

Formerly known as Spike's disease. CECS is seen in Border Terriers starting between two and six years of age. It is characterised by seizure-like symptoms, loss of balance and muscle spasm, but without any loss of consciousness. Often there is abdominal tensing with loud intestinal noises, exaggerated stretching and trembling.

The duration of episodes varies from a few seconds to 20 minutes, often worsening each time, and with and a reduced time gap between episodes.

The cause is unknown but it appears to have an hereditary component and is generally thought of as a neurological disorder. It is often seen in a number of dogs from the same litter, with no discrimination between males and females. Response to treatment is often poor but a low protein diet may be beneficial.

Investigations are on-going to find the cause of this disease, and to find ways of managing it and treating it. Affected Border Terriers should be eliminated from breeding programmes, and littermates should be carefully monitored.

HEREDITARY CATARACTS

There is some evidence that Border Terriers may be affected by this inherited condition.

A cataract is an opacity in the lens of the eye, classically with a milky white appearance. A dog with developing cataracts may first have problems with night vision. But this will develop to full blindness over time.

Cataracts may be hereditary; they could be caused by ageing, and by some diseases associated with elderly dogs such as diabetes. Physical injury or trauma to the eye could also play a part. Obviously, this makes it difficult to develop a coherent picture of what is going on in the breed. Breeders are advised to research bloodlines thoroughly, including dogs that have been

Complementary therapies should be used alongside conventional medicine.

affected by late-onset cataracts.

LEGG-CALVE PERTHES DISEASE (LCPD)

This is a disease found primarily in terrier breeds. It involves a lack of blood supply to the head of the femur (part that interacts with the pelvis) resulting in the death of bone cells in that area. The dead bone cells cause damage to the covering cartilage and there is often ensuing inflammation or arthritis.

The cause of LCPD is not known, but it is thought to have an hereditary component and an increased risk in any disease that reduces blood flow.

Clinical signs are lameness and pain in one or both back legs, usually seen in dogs less than 12 months of age. Diagnosis will involve veterinary examination and then X-rays taken under anaesthetic.

Treatment varies depending on the degree of damage. Mild disease may be managed with pain relief and rest, whereas severe disease often requires surgery.

SHAKING PUPPY SYNDROME

Spongiform Leuco Encephalo Myelopathy (SLEM), also known as shaking puppy syndrome is a recently reported issue in the breed. There is some thought that there may be a link with CECS – Canine epileptoid cramping syndrome (see page 144) but this has yet to be proven.

The condition, which involves uncoordinated tremors in puppies, is a known gene mutation in Weimaraners. In Border Terriers, onset appears to be slightly later and puppies seem to improve as they mature.

There is a DNA test available which detects if an individual is clear, affected, or a carrier of the disease.

COMPLEMENTARY THERAPIES

Just as for human health, I do believe that there is a place for alternative therapies alongside and complementing orthodox treatment under the supervision of a veterinary surgeon. Because animals do not have a choice, there are measures in place to safeguard their wellbeing and welfare. All manipulative treatment (e.g. physiotherapy) must be under the direction of a veterinary surgeon. All other complementary therapies, such as acupuncture, homoeopathy and aromatherapy, can only be carried out by veterinary surgeons who have been trained in that particular field.

ACUPUNCTURE

Acupuncture is mainly used in pain relief, often to good effect. The needles look more alarming to the owner, but they are very fine and are well tolerated by most canine patients. Speaking personally, superficial needling is not unpleasant and does help with pain relief.

HOMOEOPATHY

Homoeopathy has had a mixed press in recent years. It is based on the concept of treating like with like. Additionally, a homoeopathic remedy is said to become more powerful the more it is diluted.

CONCLUSION

As the owner of a Border Terrier, you are responsible for his care and health. Not only must you make decisions on his behalf, you are also responsible for establishing a lifestyle for him that will ensure he leads a long and happy life. Diet plays as important a part in this as does exercise. For the domestic dog, it is only in recent years that the need has been recognised for changing the diet to suit the dog as he grows, matures and then enters his twilight years. So-called life-stage diets try to match the nutritional needs of the dog as he progresses through life.

An adult dog food will suit the Border Terrier living a standard family life. There are also foods for those Border Terriers tactfully termed as obese-prone, such as those who have been neutered or are less active than others, or simply like their food. Do remember that ultimately you are in control of your Border Terrier's diet, unless he is able to profit from scavenging! On the other hand, prescription diets are of necessity fed under the supervision of a veterinary surgeon because each is formulated to meet the very specific needs of particular health conditions. Should a prescription diet be fed to a healthy dog, or to a dog with a different illness, there could be adverse effects.

It is important to remember that your Border Terrier has no choice. As his owner, you are responsible for any decision made, so it must be as informed a decision as possible. Always speak to your veterinary surgeon if you have any worries about your Border Terrier. He is not just a dog; he will become a definite member of the family from the moment you bring him home.

THE CONTRIBUTORS

THE EDITOR
BETTY JUDGE (PLUSHCOURT)

Betty was born into a farming family and has been involved with livestock as long as she can remember. She has achieved Top National and International success with her show ponies and horses before turning her attention to dogs. Betty started in Border Terriers with the best bloodlines and dogs she could source at that time; all the dogs at Plushcourt go back to the five original Border Terriers she started with. She has made up a total of 11 British Champions, the first born in 1982, some of which are multi-titled, including a Group Championship Show Terrier Group winner and a World Champion title in 1994, with many other Border Terriers winning Challenge Certificates. The latest Border to be made up into a Champion was at the 2008 Crufts Dog Show.

There are approximately 25 other Champion Border Terriers worldwide from the Plushcourt kennel. Two Petits Bassets Griffons Vendeens hold British titles, one of which also holds a World title and third in the group at the World Dog Show in Milan in 2000 and is winner of a Hound Group that same year, with others winning Challenge Certificates, and several Worldwide Champions.

Added to the kennel in 2002, was the Portuguese Podengo, and Betty brought the first dogs to the UK and got them recognised with the Kennel Club. At present this breed does not yet have Challenge Certificates, but in the meantime

she has travelled Europe to show them, and in only five years, has 18 Champions to her name, several who are multi-titled.

Betty is a member of the Kennel Club, a committee member of the Southern Border Terrier Club for over 15 years, and chairman of the Portuguese Podengo Club of Great Britain. She is an approved Kennel Club Championship Show judge of the Border Terrier, and judges all the other Terrier breeds and hound breeds at Open Shows.
See Chapter Seven: The Perfect Border Terrier.

MARIE SHARP (RHOZZUM)

Marie's first Border Terrier was born in 1970, and he set her off on a lifetime of involvement with the breed. Over the last 25 years she has had first-hand experience of traditional terrier work in terrain that is very similar to Border Hunt country. Most of her Borders have been out with the local hunt, mixing amicably with hounds, terriers and strangers, but sidelined in favour of white terriers when it comes to terrier work.

Marie judges Border Terriers and has awarded Challenge Certificates on 11 occasions, the first being in 1984. In the show ring, three Champions have carried the Rhozzum name (plus many more overseas). Ch. Rhozzum Columbo was the Top Stud Dog in the breed 2006 (*Our Dogs* table), and is the sire of Ch. Brumberhill Betwixt, top-winning bitch of all time. Many Rhozzums have been exported and have done well in Australia, Denmark, Finland, Norway,

France, and the Netherlands. International Champions Rhozzum Night Owl and Rhozzum Victor were both Show and Working Champions in Denmark.
See Chapter One: Getting to Know Border Terriers.

TRAK FRYER (IRTON)

Trak and her husband, Dave, have been breeding Champion Border Terriers for 20 years and are both Championship Show judges. They have lived and worked in the Lake District for nearly 40 years, and their early interest in the breed came about because they were looking for a tough, hardy little dog that could accompany them on long walks on the Fells. Having acquired a Border Terrier, they got involved with showing at local Hunt Terrier and Open shows.

They acquired their first show quality dog from Bertha Sullivan, of the world famous Dandyhow kennels, who lives in nearby West Cumbria. This was Dandyhow April Fool, who became their first Champion and lived to the great age of 17 years. Since then Trak and Dave have bred or made up eight Border Terrier Champions, with a number of other CC winners as well as a few overseas Champions.

The Irton kennel has never been large kennel – no more than 10 Borders are kept at a time, and a litter is only bred when a new generation is needed for the show-ring. The Irton Borders have always been "dogs first and show dogs second", so Trak and Dave have enjoyed many happy hours walking with them on the Fells, simply enjoying their company or repairing their depredations in the garden!

Living with Borders has inspired Trak's interest in the history and development of the breed; she has been the lucky recipient of much Border history and lore from those who have been involved in the breed for many decades.

Trak has been the 'Breed Notes' writer in the national dog press for a number of years, and currently serves as chairman of the Northern Border Terrier Club, one of the oldest of the UK Clubs.
See Chapter Two: The First Border Terriers.

KATHY WILKINSON (OTTERKIN)
Kathy had her first Border Terrier in November 1980, and Max (Sutoby Bright as a Button) was a constant companion and loyal friend for 16 years. She became interested in showing, and Kizzy (Sutoby Foxy Lady of Otterkin) won her first Challenge Certificate.

Since those early days, the Otterkin kennel has been blessed with some lovely dogs to own and show and has made up, bred or owned, seven UK Champions, along with other Champions in the USA and Holland.

Kathy served on the committee of the Northern Border Terrier Club for 20 years acting as assistant secretary, and later secretary. She is currently honorary secretary of the parent club, The Border Terrier Club. Kathy judges Border Terriers at Championship level; she has awarded CCs in the UK on nine occasions, including Crufts in March 2007. She has

also judged in Holland, Sweden, Denmark, Finland and at a two day Specialty in the USA.
See Chapter Three: A Border Terrier for your Lifestyle; Chapter Four: The New Arrival.

LESLEY GOSLING (AKENSIDE)
Lesley lives in the Border Terrier heartland of rural Northumbria and has more than 30 years' experience in the breed, having worked her dogs to fox with local Foxhound packs and shown them successfully at both Kennel Club and Hunt Terrier shows. She has bred and exported Borders to Australia, Canada, America, Austria, Germany and the Czech Republic.

Lesley was the Border Terrier Breed Notes writer for a number of years for *Dog World*, and is a member of several of the seven UK Border Terrier Clubs as well as serving on the Northern Border Terrier Club committee and acting as its press officer.

Lesley is a Championship show judge of Borders and has judged the breed in the UK, Sweden, the Czech Republic and twice in America. She believes passionately that new owners should be fully aware and understand the working heritage of the breed, which gives it its own particular features and characteristics, whether they are looking for a companion dog, a show dog or a worker.
See Chapter Five: The Best of Care.

JULIA BARNES
Julia has owned and trained a number of different dog breeds, and is a puppy socialiser for Dogs for the Disabled. A former journalist, she has written many

books, including several on dog training and behaviour.

Julia is indebted to SUE PICKERIN HNC (Canine Behaviour and Training) Fd SC (Canine Behaviour and Training) Associate Member of the British Institute of Professional Dog Trainers (BIPDT) for her specialist knowledge on Border Terriers. Sue has shown and bred Border Terriers for 25 years, and has made up three Champions. She also judges Border Terriers at Championship level. Sue has competed in working trials, gaining CDEx with Borders and up to WD with her German Shepherd Dog. She competes in Agility with Sally, her Border Terrier, at grade 5 level.
See Chapter Six: Training and Socialisation.

ALISON LOGAN MA VetMB MRCVS
Alison qualified as a veterinary surgeon from Cambridge University in 1989, having been brought up surrounded by all manner of animals and birds in the north Essex countryside. She has been in practice in her home town ever since, living with her husband, two children and Labrador Retriever Pippin.

She contributes on a regular basis to *Veterinary Times, Veterinary Nurse Times, Dogs Today, Cat World* and *Pet Patter,* the PetPlan newsletter. In 1995, Alison won the Univet Literary Award with an article on Cushing's Disease, and she won it again (as the Vetoquinol Literary Award) in 2002, writing about common conditions in the Shar-Pei.
See Chapter Eight: Happy and Healthy.